Bob Hope's
Confessions of a Hooker:
My Lifelong Love Affair with Golf

BOB HOPE'S

Confessions of a Hooker:
My Lifelong
Love Affair with Golf
By Bob Hope
As told to Dwayne Netland

DOUBLEDAY & COMPANY, INC., GARDEN CITY, NEW YORK   1987

For the many pictures in this book we are deeply grateful to the fine photographers who have followed my career through the years, including staff members of *Look* magazine, NASA, the U.S. Navy, the U.S. Air Force, the Los Angeles *Times,* the Washington *Post,* the White House, the Australian Photographic Agency, NBC, and the Cunard Line; also thanks to Zeni Photography, Amy Sancetta of the Columbus *Dispatch,* Alfred Trerotola, Maurice Miller, Herb Ball, Alex J. Morrison, L. P. Thomas and D. Cronen, Hugh Morton, Max Kolin, Julian Graham, Fred Sabine, Talstem Photography, Richard C. Briggs, Frank Carroll, Peter Koelman of the Union-Tribune Publishing Company, Fred Vance, Bill Knight, Hank Cohen and the Press Bureau, Delray Beach, and Steve Szurlej.

Designed by Laurence Alexander
Trade Paperback Edition, 1987

Library of Congress Cataloging in Publication Data
Hope, Bob, 1903–
    Bob Hope's Confessions of a Hooker

    1. Golf—Anecdotes, facetiae, satire, etc.
I. Netland, Dwayne.   II. Title.

GV967.H54   1985   796.352'0207   84-24665

ISBN: 0-385-17442-X
ISBN: 0-385-18896-X (pbk.)

Printed in the United States of America
15   14   13   (hc)
9   8   7   6   5   4   3   2   1   (pbk.)

Acknowledgments

The list of people who need to be thanked for this book is deeper than Bob Hope's thirst for a flawless round of golf. While the book is essentially a collaboration between Bob and myself, so many have contributed in vital ways behind the scenes, such as Bob's wife Dolores, who was most helpful in assembling the names of persons involved with the Bob Hope Desert Classic, together with other aspects of the Classic. I'm also indebted to four others associated with the tournament—General Bill Yancey, the former executive secretary; his able successor, Ed Heoreodt; Paul Jenkins, one of the key forces in the Classic; and Cliff Brown, an old friend who has been the Classic's publicity director from the onset.

From Bob's own staff, I'm grateful to Ward Grant, Wyn Hope, Carol Shaw, Kathy Schroeder and Mark Anthony. The same goes for Scorpy Doyle, the Tamarisk starter and a former Lakeside caddie; Bob's pal Jack Hennessy; Allan Kalmus and Joe Goldstein, who do public relations work for Bob in New York; Terry McKeown, a young fan of Bob in New York who came up with some much-appreciated research; and Bill Fugazy, the New York transportation man who was instrumental in coordinating many efforts.

I'll always be appreciative for the many favors of Norman Blackburn, the Lakeside historian; Jim Martin of Birmingham, Alabama; Admiral Alan Shepard; photographers Amy Sansetta, Fred Vance, and Bill Knight for their special contributions; two of my esteemed colleagues of the press, Dave Anderson of The New York *Times* and golf essayist Herbert Warren Wind for their sage suggestions; Bob and Betty Brothen, at whose home I stayed while working with Bob in Palm Springs; and my wife Joanne, who contributed substantially in the preparation of the manuscript.

The genesis of the book took place during a discussion with Bill Davis, founder and editor in chief of *Golf Digest,* and Dick Simon of D'Arcy-Masius-MacManus at the *Golf Digest* house in Augusta, Georgia, during the Masters Tournament a few years ago. Nick Seitz, *Golf Digest*'s editorial director, provided helpful encouragement and Bob took it from there.

Arnold Palmer, Jack Nicklaus, Tom Watson, Lee Trevino and Billy Casper all took time from their busy schedules to offer the comments on the jacket flap, and no words can express my gratitude to Gerald Ford for his poignantly worded Foreword.

I'm delighted that Doubleday & Company, Inc., is the publisher of the book and I want to thank four people there who were most responsible for its production—Nelson Doubleday; Ferris Mack, long one of Doubleday's top editors; his successor, Harold Kuebler; and their assistants, Lani Mysak and Judy Ganeles. Ferris retired recently after fifty years at Doubleday, and came in to the office afterward on numerous occasions to work on the editing. Ferris, a wonderful man, doesn't play golf. But for years he kept a golf ball in the pocket of his overcoat to ensure a proper identification of the garment in the checkrooms of the New York restaurants where he regularly lunched.

I've saved my warmest thanks for last—to Bob, for his gracious and vigorous collaboration. He blocked out extended periods of his around-the-clock schedule to work on the book. We spent many long hours together, taping the dialogue and reviewing the manuscript. His energy and attention to details were astonishing. We would be carefully going over a segment of say, the Ike chapter, and Bob would say, "It doesn't quite play right this way. Let's add some new material, delete this paragraph and move these two paragraphs up." And back I'd go for more revisions. In the meantime, Bob was donating his entire fee from this book to the USO.

We worked hard and we had a lot of fun, in Los Angeles, Palm Springs, St. Louis, Columbus, Westchester, Green Bay, New York and on flights across the country. Nearly every day of collaboration was culminated by a round of golf, at Lakeside, Canyon, Eldorado, Old Warson and other delightful courses. Bob's love of golf is deep and genuine, and his contributions to the game over half a century are inestimable.

I think that love is reflected in the pages of this book. It's Bob's story, and he tells it with his heart on his sleeve.

Dwayne Netland

Contents

Foreword

Writing a Foreword for a book about golf by Bob Hope may be the only way for me to get a word in edgewise or otherwise. I'd like to think that being a former President of the United States is something special. Not to Hope. I'm just another target for his sandbagging bets on the course and his big laughs on the stage.

I don't want anyone to get the impression that Bob Hope is anything other than my very dear friend. We play golf together often. I win, he wins; I lose, he loses; I pay, he tells a joke! In spite of all the wonderful gifts and mementos given me, if I could have one special piece of memorabilia, it would be the first dollar Bob Hope ever paid on a bet lost on a golf course. The search for that bill wouldn't be difficult. It's still in Bob's right-hand pants pocket.

Having sat in the hot seat in the White House, I can tell you that the press corps in Washington can give you a pretty good "working over." The treatment they gave me was nothing compared to what Hope says about me. For example, he says, "There are forty-two golf courses in the Palm Springs area and nobody knows which one Ford is playing until after he hits his tee shot!" Or, "It's not hard to find Jerry Ford on a golf course, you just follow the wounded!" The one he especially enjoys is "Jerry Ford has made golf a contact sport."

Of course I want to be fair and say that Bob Hope is very even-handed when dispensing his sharp-edged humor. Democrats John Kennedy and Lyndon Johnson didn't get any more or less of his hilarious one-liners than Dwight Eisenhower or Jerry Ford. I wouldn't dare to repeat what he says about Tip O'Neill!

Bob comes up each year to the Jerry Ford Invitational held in Vail, Colorado. At Vail's altitude of 8,200 feet his drives go fifty yards farther than usual. He thinks he's twenty-five years old again and starts to make some ridiculous comments about going on the tour. If I could only get him instantly down to sea level, I know I could recoup all my money in one round. But that would mean I outsmarted him and I don't think I'm capable of that, at least not where golf is concerned. What's more, even if I could, I wouldn't want to. Bob Hope should always come out on top as far as

What could be sweeter? Former President Gerald Ford dusting off the mothballs to pay me off for the nassau in our appearance of the pro-am of the Memorial Tournament in 1983. You don't get the President in this situation too often, and I can tell you it was beautiful.

Presidents and former Presidents are concerned. It's good for people to hear what he says and he knows how to say it to get the laugh, make a point and not be too hurtful. Being able to do that is a gift that belongs to his audiences and should never be tampered with because of the egos of Presidents or anyone else. Not that we're not important. After all, where would Bob Hope be today without "old, out-of-work politicians" who keep trying to master the game of golf under public scrutiny?

Bob and I have a lot in common. We both obviously love the game, its challenge, frustration, camaraderie and beauty. We both travel, probably more than we should or need to, but don't seem to tire of it. We both have our roots near the Great Lakes and found our way to Southern California. And, we both have run out of excuses or explanations for Betty and Dolores as to why the lure of the links still is like a siren's call to both of us. It's the only love affair either one of those great women would ever condone. In thinking about why Dolores and Betty put up with us, I remember a wonderful line by Hubert Humphrey, "Some women marry below themselves." Hubert was a dear friend who probably would have been able to handle Hope for me. Unfortunately, Hubert didn't play golf.

Everyone might think of Bob as "Mr. Comedy," but if you talked to people over the last six decades, people like Byron Nelson, Sam Snead, Gary Player, Arnold Palmer, Lee Trevino, Jack Nicklaus, Tom Watson and many others, they would say the title of "Mr. Golf" is just as appropriate. This book very clearly pulls together Bob's credentials for the title.

It should be evident that golf, and especially golf with Bob Hope, has given me as much enjoyment, relaxation and laughter as anything else in my life. Golf is a great game that has grown because of the many purposes it serves. Bob Hope has contributed immeasurably to the good things golf can provide. His Desert Classic has raised millions of dollars for charities and has become a model for other charitable tournaments held around the country.

I'm just one person on the long list of Presidents and former Presidents Bob Hope has known and taken to task with his golf and humor. But there's only one Bob Hope and I'm very proud to have the determined, smooth-swinging golfer as a buddy. I know he'll shoot his age, even if he has to live to be 125 to do it! I've enjoyed the book, I know you will.

Gerald R. Ford

One

My First Caddie Wasn't Really a Dinosaur

Golf is such a great game. When you get out there and commune with nature on those beautiful courses like Pebble Beach, Cypress Point, Capilano in Vancouver with that glorious view from the tees, Deepdale and Meadow Brook with the Long Island Sound in the background, the desert courses with the mountains looming just off the green fairways . . . well, it's just fantastic being out there.

I've been playing golf a long time, although it's not really true that on my first round they strapped my bag on the back of a dinosaur. I've been at the game for fifty-five years, and a little more if you count my first aborted stab at it. It's a big part of my life. I hardly ever travel without my golf clubs, which means that I stick pretty close to Los Angeles and Palm Springs during the winter months. But in 1983 for some reason I did five shows in Minneapolis in March. We got hit by two blizzards. I had to kick away the snow to open the stage door at the theater. After getting home I went to the Eisenhower Medical Center to have my head examined.

The first time I tried golf I was a total failure. I went out for a few rounds in 1927, when I was twenty-four, at Highland Park, a public course in Cleveland. I couldn't advance the ball. Some shots I'd whiff, some I'd just scuff along the ground. Foursomes of women were playing through me. I just didn't seem to have any feel for the game, so I said the hell with it and quit.

In 1930 I was on the vaudeville circuit with the Diamond Brothers, a comedy act. During the summer we played the northern route—Winnipeg, Calgary, Minneapolis, Seattle and Tacoma. We did matinees and evening shows, so there was nothing for me to do during the morning except sit around the hotel lobbies. I used to see the Diamonds come clattering through the lobby every day with their golf bags. One day, in Seattle, they invited me to come along. I borrowed a set of clubs and started hitting the ball pretty well. I got hooked on golf that day. I've been addicted to it ever since.

My wife Dolores loves the game, too, and she has always been a competent player. She has a record at the Lakeside Golf Club in North Hollywood, California, that may never be eclipsed—five times the women's club runner-up, never the champion. I've kidded her a lot about that over the years.

My handicap today is twenty and I'm comfortable with that, but at one time, in the early 1950s, I had it down to 6. It actually was a 4 for one week in 1951, when I went over to play in the British Amateur at Porthcawl in Wales. But that's another story.

I get upset over a bad shot just like anyone else. But it's silly to let the game get to you. When I miss a shot I just think what a beautiful day it is. And what pure fresh air I'm breathing. Then I take a deep breath. I have to do that. That's what gives me the strength to break the club.

We used to have some pretty fancy tournaments at Lakeside. Nothing like getting dressed up for a Sunday round.

But isn't golf a wonderful game? Just the other day I was sitting in the locker room at Lakeside and one of my pals came stumbling in. He was so dejected. I asked him what happened in his match and he replied, "What chance did I have? He threw a 98 at me."

When people ask me how long I've been playing the game I just say that when I started the President of the United States was a man who believed you should speak softly and carry a big stick. It was the same during the Eisenhower administration, only the big stick was a 7 iron.

The man who had the biggest influence on my game in the early years was Alex Morrison. He was an extraordinarily good instructor, one of the best ever. He was also a superb showman. We appeared onstage together in New York and hit those papier-mâché balls out into the audience. Alex had a driving range under the Fifty-ninth Street bridge. I'd go there often for lessons. He'd tell me, "Roll your feet, roll your feet." I still do it. It gets me extra distance. And at my age I need all the extra distance I can get.

From 1930 until 1937 I lived at 65 Central Park West, while I was on Broadway, and belonged to Green Meadow, up in Westchester County. I played all the courses in the New York area . . . Deepdale, Meadow Brook, Apawamis, Westchester, Winged Foot. By the time I went out to Hollywood in 1937 I was a fairly decent player. I don't know how you'd describe my swing at the time, but to some it looked a little like a polo player without a horse.

I'll always remember my days in New York. They were great times. In 1932 I got a role in a Broadway show called *Ballyhoo* and stayed on the boards for five years. The show I remember best was *Roberta.* I was in it at the time I met the woman who became Dolores Hope. Her name was Dolores Reade. She was singing at the Vogue Club. George Murphy, who was also in *Roberta,* and I were having a beer at the Lambs Club after the show one night and George asked me, "How would you like to hear a pretty girl sing?" She was gorgeous. Dolores sang "It's Only a Paper Moon" and seven or eight other lilting numbers. Murphy introduced me to her, and I invited her to see *Roberta.* She did, and then she came backstage. "I didn't know you had such a big role," she said. "I thought you were in the chorus line." We were married in 1934, in Erie, Pennsylvania.

In 1937 I signed a seven-year contract with Paramount Studios to do three pictures a year. Dolores and I took the Santa Fe Chief to Los Angeles, arriving on a sunny day in September. Not long after I joined Lakeside, located near the major studio lots, because that's where Bing Crosby played. In 1940 we bought a house that was just five minutes away from the club, and it's been my home in Los Angeles ever since, with a few major remodeling jobs.

Here's a publicity shot of my first movie, The Big Broadcast of 1938 *with W. C. Fields and Shirley Ross, that I signed for Stu Symington. I always regret never having played golf with Bill Fields.*

Lakeside was a haven for the movie crowd. You'd see everyone there . . . Howard Hughes, Jean Harlow, Ruby Keeler, Babe Hardy, Edgar Kennedy, Dick Arlen, Adolphe Menjou, Leon Errol, Randy Scott, Buddy Rogers, W. C. Fields and Johnny Weissmuller. There were also some outstanding low-handicap amateurs—Roger Kelly, Bruce McCormick, Johnny Dawson and George Von Elm.

Roger Kelly was a fabulous player. In those days he was also a man with a prodigious thirst. His drinking bouts were legendary. One day Roger and I went down to Palm Springs and played O'Donnell, a very fine course. Roger had a terrible hangover. He shot the first 9 in 52, sobered up and did the back 9 in 34. Later he stopped drinking completely. Today he's still one of the finest players at Lakeside.

The motion picture companies shot most of their golf footage at Lakeside in my early years there. Bobby Jones, who retired from tournament golf after winning the Grand Slam in 1930, was often on the scene working on his instructional movies. In my first film, *The Big Broadcast of 1938,* W. C. Fields had some hilarious golf scenes on the course.

Fields portrayed two characters in the movie, S. B. Bellows, a millionaire shipowner, and his brother T. Frothington Bellows, a troublemaker. Fields played the golf course in a motor scooter, if you can believe that. He lived just across Toluca Lake from the club, and we used to see him sometimes in the mornings in his pajamas, chasing the ducks off his yard.

The Big Broadcast of 1938 is still very special to me. Directed by Mitchell Leisen, it contained a musical number I did with Shirley Ross, a lovely song called "Thanks for the Memory." It became my theme, following me all over the world.

I never played golf with Bill Fields, but I heard many stories about the way he used to ham it up on the course. Norm Blackburn, in his book commemorating Lakeside's fiftieth anniversary, recalled that one day on the 1st tee Fields whiffed his drive. He said, "Saaay, one of my better shots," and headed down the fairway. About two hundred yards out he instructed his caddie, Scorpy Doyle, to drop another ball. "Oh, here it is," Fields said. "Mighty fine drive." Nobody seemed to mind. He was just being Bill Fields, and there was nobody else like him.

I didn't spend all my time making pictures and playing golf during those early Hollywood days. Eddie Lasker, a fine player at the Century Club in Westchester, whose father Albert ran a big advertising agency in Chicago, encouraged me to go on the radio. Pepsodent sponsored the show from 1934 to 1950, and later I did some television work for Pepsodent.

Those radio shows were fun. Bing had his own program at the time, sponsored by Kraft, and we'd trade guest spots every now and then, usually with a golf routine included somewhere in the show.

It was about this time, maybe a couple of years later, that I met two of golf's real characters, Jimmy Demaret and Toney Penna. We became pals, and it was truly a sad day for me when Jimmy died in December of 1983. He and Jackie Burke owned and ran the Champions Golf Club in Houston. Toney was one of the finest golf club designers of all time. He worked for MacGregor, and had his own company for a long time before finally deciding to retire.

Demaret, very good on his feet, once introduced me with the line "Bob's got a great short game. Unfortunately it's off the tee."

Penna could not only design golf clubs, he could play. On one round he instructed his caddie to watch the flight of the ball after he had swung. Toney hit a fine shot and asked the caddie where it went. "I don't know," said the caddie. "I marked it with those birds, but they flew away."

Doug Sanders became sort of a latter-day Demaret, with his boulevardier life-style and flashy wardrobe. Doug once told me of the time in a pro-am when he was paired with a particularly wild amateur who spent most of the round looking for his ball in the woods.

Walking down the 12th fairway the amateur encountered a friend who had hit his shot over onto the 12th from the 14th. Asked which pro he was playing with, the wild swinger said, "I don't know. I haven't met him yet."

I still play in several pro-ams on the PGA Tour each year in addition to the Desert Classic, but most of my golf at Lakeside these days is over the 9-hole route. I'll drive over in the late afternoon to hit a few balls and get in a quick 9. Dolores and I often play together on Sunday afternoons. I play more just for the enjoyment.

I'm just kidding. I play better than that, usually in the low 90s if I go the full 18. But golf's a hard game to figure. One day you'll go out and slice it, shank it, hit into all the traps and miss every green. The next day you go out and for no reason at all you really stink.

But occasionally it all comes together. Dolores and I played once in Vienna, at a golf course on the inside of a racetrack. You could stop and watch the horses and see how your money was doing, and then continue playing. Anyway, I played the course on Saturday and did pretty well. Dolores went out for her round the next day. When she had finished, one of the members stood up on the steps of the clubhouse and grandly announced, "Scores: Mr. Bob Hope, 79; Mrs. Bob Hope, 78." Dolores got a kick out of that.

One of nature's true golf masterpieces is Pine Valley, at Clementon, New Jersey, where I have an honorary membership. It's an awesome blend of turf, sand, scrubland, trees and water. The first time I ever saw it I shot a 103, with a 10 on a par-3 hole. I had bet my old friend Chris Dunphy I could break 90. I agreed to pay him $10 for every shot over 90. He collected

My pal Jimmy Demaret and I clowning it up, as usual, during the Texas Open during the mid-1950s. Jimmy was one of a kind, a special guy. We all lost a great friend when he died in December of 1983.

on me that day. But a few years later I had 84, which is a pretty darn good score at Pine Valley. Foursomes have left the 1st tee there and have never been seen again. They just find their shoelaces and bags.

Speaking of Chris Dunphy, he was quite a guy. Chris was in the promotion department at Paramount when I got there in 1937. Then he moved East and joined the original Deepdale, out on Long Island. The club that had the big calcutta scandal. Somebody got in a member-guest there one year with a phony handicap and picked up a bundle. They never saw that fellow around Deepdale again.

During the winter Chris spent a lot of time at Seminole, in North Palm Beach, Florida. Beautiful place. Great course, and one of the finest men's locker rooms you'll see anywhere. The place just reeks with golf atmosphere. They've got those plaques on the wall with the names of the various club tournament winners on them. Crosby's name is there. So is Ben Hogan's. I don't see much chance of Hope ever making it.

Dunphy, who had become chairman of the club, invited John Kennedy down to play when Kennedy was President. On the first hole, a par 4, Kennedy floats a nice 4-iron approach shot in there about three feet from the pin. Kennedy walks up to the ball and glances over at Chris, looking for a conceded putt. Chris ignores him, and stares up at the sky.

"You're certainly going to give me this, aren't you?" Kennedy asked.

"Make a pass at it," Dunphy replied. "I want to see your stroke. A putt like this builds character. Besides, it will give you a little feel for the greens."

Kennedy grimaced. "I work in the Oval Office all day for citizens like you," he said. "And now you're not going to give me this putt."

Dunphy stood mute.

"OK," Kennedy sighed. "But let's keep moving. I've got an appointment after we finish with the director of Internal Revenue."

"The putt's good," Dunphy said hastily. "Pick it up."

I'll never forget the first time I played with Joe Louis, the former heavyweight champion, who really loved his golf. It was a long time ago, at the Ridgewood Country Club in Ridgewood, New Jersey. Ed Sullivan and I were paired against Louis and Byron Nelson, who was pro there at the time. I was playing Joe individually for a $10 nassau.

On the 1st hole Louis had about a two-foot putt and Sullivan said, "That's good, Joe." Same thing on the 2d. On the 3d, Joe had one a little longer. Sullivan must have been trying to butter him up for an appearance on his television show. "Pick it up, Joe," Sullivan said. I stepped in and said, "Hey, wait a minute, putt that one out for me." Joe fell on the ground laughing, because he knew he'd been getting away with it.

I was at the Hollywood American Legion Club during a boxing card one night during World War II when Joe, a G.I. in the U.S. Army, was

February 9, 1944, at a War Relief outing at Lakeside. I was the only competitor in the group, but Dottie Lamour, Gary Cooper and Ginny Simms were on hand to provide a little Hollywood glamour for the war bond sales.

In the early days at Lakeside: Humble Robert with Fred Astaire, Joe Louis, Arthur
Stebbins and Jimmy McLarnin, the fighter. Louis was a helluva golfer, much better
than most people realize. His knockout punch on the course was, of course, his
driver. Oh, by the way, I made a hole in one on the day this picture was taken. I
knocked a 7-iron in on the 15th. Just a routine round.

Too bad I missed this one. But there were plenty of other hams in this Palm Beach outing—Sam Snead, Phil Harris, Bing, Chris Dunphy, and Toney Penna. I'd like to have the scorecard—and the money that changed hands—from that round.

introduced. They gave him a two-minute standing ovation. You remember his response? Joe took the microphone and said, "Thank you. We're gonna win this war cuz God's on our side."

Joe was with me when I had a hole in one at Lakeside. Joe, Fred Astaire and Jimmy McLarnin, the former welterweight champion. On the 15th hole, now the 6th, I hit 7-iron that covered the flag all the way and rolled in. We could see it from the tee. Joe looked at me and said, "Man, that went right in the hole."

One Christmas Day I was playing at Lakeside with Jack Hennessy, an old pal from Los Angeles. On the 15th, the same hole I had aced with Joe Louis, Hennessy shanked his tee shot. "I'll play another from the tee," he said. "You gonna charge me only one shot?" Imbued with the true holiday spirit, I agreed. On the next shot Jack hit it into the cup.

"Merry Christmas," I told him. "You've just made a hole in two."

Two

Hackers on Display
at the Pro-Ams

Incredible is the only word to describe the growth of one of golf's great phenomenons, the professional-amateur prelude to a tournament on the PGA or LPGA Tour. Everybody knows them as pro-ams, and not only are they a lot of fun for the participants, they're a source of large sums of money.

I'm not referring here to just the Desert Classic, where the amateurs play four days on four different courses, or the Crosby, where the amateurs play three days on three courses. I'm talking about the pro-ams that take place every week on the tours. Almost all of them are one day; several now are two. In nearly every case the money from the pro-am is enough to subsidize the entire tournament.

The usual format is four amateurs playing 18 holes on Wednesday with one of the leading pros on the money list. It's generally best ball of the group with full handicaps, the pro playing at scratch. It's never an easy task for the pro. It must be a thrill to miss a four-foot putt and have four hackers tell you what you should have done. For some reason, many amateurs like to give free advice, or solicit free tips from the pro. The pros hear "What am I doing wrong?" more times than Dolores did on our honeymoon.

Pro-ams are nothing new. They had them forty years ago on what then constituted the men's tour. I know, because I played in several back then. But they were piddling in scope to what takes place each Wednesday these days from January through October. Look at the evolution in Houston.

The Coca-Cola Houston Open is held in May at the Woodlands Country Club, just north of Houston. For the past few years they've held two pro-ams, one on the West Course and one on the East, comprising a total of 416 amateurs. The demand for spots was so great that they've added another pro-am on Monday of tournament week, for twenty-six fivesomes with 104 amateurs.

In Houston's main pro-am, the Wednesday affair with 416 amateurs, there are fifty-two pros. The first forty-two are taken off the previous year's final money list and the sponsors select another ten of their choice.

The purse for each pro-am is $7,500. The low pro gets $750 and the pro on the winning team gets $750, with the other payoffs scaled down from that. Amateur prizes are nice gifts, like crystal glass. Each gift must be valued under $350, since that is the limit of value that an amateur can accept without losing his amateur status.

The entry fee for the amateurs in Houston is—get this—$2,500 to play on the West Course (with the top pros), $1,500 on the East Course and $1,000 on Monday. For one round of golf. That comes to over $1 million. No wonder they have sterling silver ball washers.

The money is tax deductible, of course, and for it come special perks like books of tournament tickets, parking, gift bags and invitations to all the best parties. It's no wonder that many pro-ams are sold out a year in advance, with a long waiting list.

17

The amateurs are broken down by handicaps in groups of A, B, C and D and the pairings are made accordingly. So each group that the pro contends with for over five hours is composed of a very good player, one who's pretty good, another just fair and one who's thrashing around while asking the pro questions like "Should I bend my knees more?" And the pro says, "Yes . . . and pray, brother, pray!"

Most of these tournaments have various numbers of celebrities, ranging from five to twenty. The galleries flock out to see them play. The celebrities have a good time, too. Phil Harris was once 5 up on Dean Martin—and that was before they left the bar. Telly Savalas plays in several each year. It's easy to tell he's been a cop for so long . . . instead of "Fore!" he yells "Freeze!" You often see Clint Eastwood. He's easy to spot. He's the only guy on the course who carries his putter in a holster.

I play in at least a dozen tour pro-ams around the country each year. Most of the time our group has more laughs than low scores, but I have been with three winning teams. I was lucky enough to knock in a forty-foot downhill putt on the 18th hole to win with Nicklaus at Atlanta, and I was in the winner's circle twice at Phoenix, once with Palmer and once with Casper. Playing with Palmer occasionally makes me nervous. I don't mind when he criticizes my swing and my grip, but when he starts lifting me in and out of the golf cart, that's too much.

At the Memorial Tournament in Dublin, Ohio, where I participate nearly every year in the pro-am, I'm generally in the group with Gerald Ford along with the defending Memorial champion and a couple of amateurs selected by Jack Nicklaus. For several years one of them was former Ohio Governor, Jim Rhodes, an old friend of mine. The entry fee for the Memorial pro-am is $2,000. I've noticed that many foursomes stay together year after year. Burch Riber, who runs the LPGA Championship, assembled a foursome in 1976 that stayed intact for eight straight years.

Phoenix, where the pro-am entry fee is now $1,200, is another of my favorite spots. After all, I have a sentimental attachment for the Valley of the Sun, having twice been on the winning team. Sam Snead and I were often paired together. One year there was some minor international incident in Iraq—I just can't recall now what it was—and I happened to ask Sam, "What do you think of Iraq?" He looked at me and said, "I never played it. Who's the pro there?" Sam thinks Beirut is an after-shave lotion.

In the fast lane with Del Webb, Arnold Palmer and Bob Goldwater at the 1971 Phoenix Open Pro-Am, Arizona Country Club. I loved that golf course because whenever I shanked, the ball always still seemed to be in play.

Our Fearsome Fivesome at the Bogie Busters in Dayton, Ohio. Cy Laughter, who founded the tournament, is wearing the loud slacks on my right, along with Gerald Ford, Governor Jim Rhodes of Ohio and Joe Garagiola. Joe's got his golf game down to where he is shooting his old batting average.

Sam Snead, the only pro to have won official tournaments in six different decades. Sam's the Old Man River of golf, with the smoothest swing the game has ever known. He's collected more honors than de Gaulle.

Tommy Bolt, one of Snead's contemporaries, was known for his Vesuvian temperament. He used to break clubs like matchsticks, although he is one of the sweetest men in the world off the course. In one pro-am he came up to the 18th hole, and had a 135-yard shot to the green. He asked the caddie which club he should use and the caddie said a 2-iron. Bolt was incredulous. "A 2-iron for a 135-yard shot?" The caddie said, "That's the only club we have left, Mr. Bolt."

Westchester, which has 36 holes, uses them all for a big doubleheader pro-am. The West Course, where the Westchester Classic is played, has fifty-two of the top pros and 208 amateurs, the amateurs paying $1,900 each. I play in that one nearly every year, along with Dinah Shore. The 1st hole is a long par 3, a tough way to start. On one occasion everyone in our group, including Raymond Floyd, missed the green except me. I knocked it on with a 5-wood . . . and then 3-putted.

The other Westchester pro-am is held on the South Course with a shotgun start, meaning every group starts at the same time on a different tee. Manufacturers Hanover, which sponsors the Westchester Classic, encouraged the presence of women in the pro-am on the South. They have several foursomes of women, some of them guests of the bank, and the women now play from their own tees. I'm envious. I've been trying to play from the women's tees for years.

Arnold Palmer has been a frequent pro-am partner of mine at Westchester. What a golfer he is. He's the biggest crowd pleaser since the invention of the portable sanitary facilities. Arnie's really had a fabulous career in golf. He's won as much money as I've spent on lessons. He told me how I could cut eight strokes off my score . . . skip one of the par 3s. But the last time we played, Arnold was only a couple of strokes up on me. Then we went on to the 2d hole.

I've had many encounters at Westchester with Jackie Gleason, and also at the Inverrary tournament he used to sponsor. Inverrary is a lovely course on Florida's east coast, near Fort Lauderdale.

It's fun playing with Gleason. He has the only golf cart with a bartender. Have you ever seen Jackie riding around in his cart? It looks like a Goodyear blimp giving birth to a jeep. When he gets into a trap, the sand has to get out.

Nearly every tournament on the tour now has a charity recipient. That's how they get the tax-deductible feature for the amateurs, and the hundreds of volunteer workers needed to run any event. For example, the Memorial has the Columbus Children's Hospital and Columbus *Dispatch* Charities; the Western has its caddie scholarship fund; Westchester has thirteen hospitals in Westchester County; the Desert Classic has the Eisenhower Medical Foundation and thirty-nine other desert charities.

It's Gleason's tournament, so we all had to laugh at his jokes. This was at the Gleason Inverrary Classic in Lauderhill, Florida, 1976, with Jackie, myself, President Ford and Jack Nicklaus.

Billy Graham must have performed another miracle, at the Byron Nelson Classic in Dallas, 1971.

The Crosby raises considerable money for the Youth Fund of the Monterey Peninsula area, along with a college scholarship fund that Bing instituted a few years before he died. The Crosby differs from any other tournament in that it has 168 amateurs and 168 pros, who are paired by a committee headed by Nathaniel Crosby. The entry fee for amateurs was doubled in 1984, from $750 to $1,500, and the waiting list for invitations sent out by the Crosby family runs from Monterey to Manila.

The weather at the Crosby is always so chancy the family sends, with its invitations, small-craft warnings. I played in it for years with thirteen clubs and a life raft. On the 16th hole at Cypress Point I took so many mulligans I finally hired Charlie the Tuna to toss my ball back on the fairway.

It's the only tournament where they hand an amateur a score card and a computer. After playing at Hurricane Alley, the locals' name for Pebble Beach, you can play anywhere. They've had rain so many times they're thinking of holding the tournament indoors. I've often wondered what it was like to play golf inside a ball washer.

Unlike Pebble Beach, we almost always get fabulous weather for the Desert Classic, which has 408 amateurs and 136 pros. The amateur spots are sold out a year in advance. We get dozens of overseas calls from guys wanting to get in. I usually bring down about twenty of my celebrity pals, who have a terrific time and contribute substantially to the fact we have such huge galleries.

Among them is Joe Garagiola, the former baseball catcher who sponsored his own tournament in Tucson for seven years. Joe's a great guy. His head was the inspiration for Dunlop golf balls. He's the only ex-baseball player able to hit his batting average on the golf course. When Joe was playing ball, he could never hit a curve. Well, he can now. His slices are majestic. But Joe was a fine catcher. He once chased a fly ball that was caught by Dolly Parton in the stands. He spent half of the next season looking for it.

Billy Graham, our earthquake insurance, is another. It's hard to beat a guy who gets a ball out of a sand trap just by muttering a few words and looking up. Billy doesn't call it a score . . . he calls it a "reckoning." I sank a 35-foot putt against him, turned around and my caddie had turned into a pillar of salt. But I almost beat him once. I only had to sink a three-foot putt. It was right on line before a flash of lightning struck and the hole sealed up.

Perry Como, the sleeping prince, is a popular attraction. Perry's so excited about golf that sometimes he even leaves a call for the back 9. He'd be a great golfer except for one thing—he keeps dozing off in the middle of his backswing. One day we were all complimenting Perry about keeping his head down until we realized he'd fallen asleep.

Along with the men, the woman pros have experienced a tremendous growth in their pro-ams. I never quite seem to play my best in the LPGA pro-ams. Before I got out of the rough in one tournament it had turned into a shopping center. I'm not afraid of the rough and the traps, but it's so humiliating when the gallery hangs your bag in effigy. I once showed Pat Bradley my swing and said, "What do I do next?" Pat replied, "Wait till the pain dies down." When I asked Jane Blalock if I should lock my grip she said she'd rather lock my bag.

The amateur entry fee for an LPGA pro-am varies from $500 to $2,500, and the people I know consider that a great bargain. Gerald Ford and I had a super time playing in women's pro-ams until our wives discovered that provocative poster of Jan Stephenson, with the inscription PLAY A ROUND WITH ME.

Football coaches like to play in the LPGA pro-ams. They're an odd group. After 9 holes they automatically run into the locker room and pray. And I'll never again ask Don Shula how he did it. I had to spend an hour with him in the locker room watching him draw diagrams of each hole on the blackboard.

One time I even played with a sheik from Kuwait, who had thirty wives. I wonder how *he* kept score.

Three

Gleason Putts
with a Swizzle Stick

I never dreamed when I took up golf that someday I'd be playing with kings and presidents, actors and singers, television stars and generals, corporate tycoons, athletes and club owners. People like Bing Crosby, Dwight Eisenhower, Gerald Ford, Clint Eastwood, Hal Linden, Ernie Borgnine, Don Rickles, Jim Garner, Bob Newhart, Sammy Davis, Jr., Flip Wilson, Tip O'Neill, Andy Williams and so many others. Golf is a bond that has drawn us all together and created a special fraternity among the celebrities of show business, sports and politics.

Jackie Gleason and I have played for a little money here and there. Jackie's such a generous man that he donated a sweater to charity as a pro-am prize and now there's a family of refugees living in it. A few years ago he had a big heart transplant in Chicago, a five-hour operation. It took the doctors four hours to get him on the operating table.

Before the surgery a nurse came into his room to get a urine specimen. Jackie was drinking beer. When the nurse left the room Jackie filled the specimen cup with beer. She picked it up and was shocked because she'd never seen one with a head on it. She called the doctor, who thought it looked rather cloudy. Jackie grabbed the cup and said, "Well, let's run it through again."

Gleason's the only golfer I know with a spigot on his 5-iron. I have two rules in golf: never play in lightning, and never cross a footbridge with Gleason. I don't know anyone else who putts with a swizzle stick.

Danny Thomas, who does so much for charity with his Memphis tournament, is one of our religious guys. He puts holy water in all the ball washers. Danny has the only golf cart I've seen with stained-glass windows.

In a way, Danny reminds me of Billy Graham. I've played many rounds with Billy. We're a lot alike. He prays and I cheat. He cheats in his own pious way. I mean how would you like to play 18 holes and have it raining just on you? He always wins, but then look at the help he's got. Pretty hard to beat a guy who gets the ball out of a sand trap just by muttering a few words and looking up.

One of my favorite pro-ams is at the Sammy Davis, Jr. Greater Hartford Open. Sammy tries to play in it, but he has a tough time. After every shot the caddie stuffs him back into the bag.

It's fun playing with Dean Martin at Riviera in Los Angeles. When he wins anything we always tell him. Dean doesn't drink liquor anymore. He drinks Windex. He gets an awful hangover but his eyes are so clear.

Fred Waring, who spent most of his active life in golf, never used irons. He had a bagful of woods. One day we were supposed to play at Bermuda Dunes but Fred didn't show up. When I called to ask him why, he said his clubs had developed termites.

Walter Annenberg is probably the smartest golfer I know. He never has to worry about starting times because he has his own private course, in Palm Springs. So does Willie Nelson, down in Austin, Texas. Willie has a big sign at the entrance that says CLOSED whenever he's in town. When he's not there, the sign comes down and all the neighbors come over and play. That's beautiful.

I have a reciprocal agreement with Andy Williams: he plays in my tournament and I play in his. Torrey Pines is a lovely setting for his event in San Diego, but occasionally the weather gets a little strong. I was playing with Al Geiberger when the wind started howling and the next thing I knew he was flying out over the Pacific on a hang glider. Andy's a sweetheart, although he can be distracting to play with. Have you ever tried to pitch over a water hazard while your partner is humming "Moon River"?

I've always enjoyed my rounds with Gene Cernan, the astronaut. Every time he sees a rock he examines it, numbers it and puts it into a bag. When Gene came down to play in the Classic for the first time, he was checking into his hotel when the bellman almost got a hernia. Gene's valise had a change of underwear, a toothbrush and two hundred pounds of rocks.

Lawrence Welk is a fine golfer. He always winds up with the best score . . . a 1 and a 2. Lawrence is the only golfer on the course with his gallery doing the polka.

Eddie Arcaro plays in a lot of the celebrity tournaments. He does great on the greens . . . although I never knew it was legal to putt with a whip.

Michael Jackson and I have a lot in common. I did a commercial for Geritol and my girdle caught on fire.

I won't mention the name of the celebrity who was playing at Gleneagles in Scotland, and taking a drink at every tee. On the 4th hole it started to rain, and on the 7th hole the guy looked at the caddie and said, "Aren't there any dry spots around here?" The caddie replied, "Well, you could start with the back of my throat."

Speaking of tippling on the course, the great Bobby Jones was known to nip a shot of whiskey every now and then. After his tournament rounds he liked to lie in his bathtub with a double or two. I had the pleasure of playing with Bobby at his home club in Atlanta, East Lake, not long before he had to give up the game because of a crippling bone disease. On the 1st hole he hit his drive out of bounds, reloaded and wheeled around the course in 68. During World War II Bobby appeared on my radio show while he was

Life's full of shocking moments when you tee it up with Gleason. This time the gallery saved me from a swoon, at the Desert Classic in 1975.

in the Army Air Force. He sent me a picture from St. Andrews and I had it on my dressing room wall at Paramount for nineteen years. What a wonderful gentleman he was, and today his legacy to golf is perpetuated in the Masters Tournament.

Humphrey Bogart was a low-handicap golfer, although for some reason not many people remember that. The last time I saw Bogey it was in my hotel room in England. He and Lauren Bacall were returning home from doing USO shows in Italy. We started drinking, and pretty soon Bogey suggested I lie down on the floor. He wanted to tee up a ball on a piece of gum on my nose and take a swat at it with my driver. And I let him do it. I haven't been able to breathe properly since that time. But it was fun.

One of the most legendary golfing celebrities of all time was Howard Hughes. He was a member at Lakeside when I joined in 1937, and also belonged to Bel-Air. Years ago there was a story going around Hollywood that when he sold TWA for $650 million, he carried the check around in his wallet for six months. I really wonder if that was true.

One Hughes story that I can vouch for is the time he called Lakeside early one evening, about ten minutes after the club's switchboard was closed. The call was taken in the men's grill by Norm Blackburn, the Lakeside historian and a delightful guy. When the phone at the bar rang, Norm picked it up and was astonished to hear this voice say, "This is Howard Hughes. Is Del Webb around?"

Hughes had been in seclusion for years, and hardly anyone had seen him. Blackburn was startled, of course, but he said, "Well, I'll look and see." Norm put the phone down and checked the locker room, the dining room and even took a quick look around the parking lot. He returned to the phone and said, "Howard, I don't believe he's here."

Hughes said, "Who is this?"

"This is Norman Blackburn."

"I remember you. I played golf with you once several years ago. You have a son in the advertising business in Honolulu. Listen, you were very kind to take all the time looking for Del. I appreciate that. Let's chat for a while."

They talked for nearly an hour.

During his Lakeside days Hughes had played often with George Von Elm, a former U.S. Amateur champion. They played three times a week for a $500 bet, and Hughes lost consistently. One day he beat Von Elm, and George got a little testy as he wrote out the check. He griped about the bad breaks he had that day, and indicated that Hughes had been lucky to win. Hughes tore up the check, looked Von Elm in the eye and said, "George, I guess we better not play anymore." Von Elm had thrown away a $1,500 weekly annuity.

Here's my own Victory Caravan—two motorcycle patrol officers escorting me in style off the course at the Capitol City club in Atlanta. I add reluctantly that Bing and Ed Dudley beat Johnny Bulla and myself 2 and 1 in an exhibition before what was then the largest gallery in Atlanta golf history.

One day Hughes had a one o'clock game scheduled at Bel-Air with Katie Hepburn. Katie got there at noon and waited for Hughes to arrive. They were taking bets that Howard wouldn't show, but at precisely five minutes to one a private plane landed on a fairway at Bel-Air and Hughes stepped out, ready to play. After 9 holes, Howard discovered that his plane had been chained to the ground and the club had imposed a $2,000 fine for landing on a fairway. Howard wrote out the check and finished the round.

Hughes, who always operated on the top level, had purchased the RKO studio and all the RKO theaters across the country for $9 million. Then he sold the theaters for $9 million and kept the studio. Not a bad deal.

He was an outstanding player, and very vain about his golf. He took a series of intensive lessons from Willie Hunter, who was the golf pro at Riviera in Los Angeles. After three frenzied months of working with Hunter, Howard approached him one day and said, "Willie, am I good enough to win the U.S. Amateur?" Hunter replied, "No, Howard, you are not."

With that, Hughes gave up the game and never played again.

Johnny Bench, who recently retired after a great baseball career with the Cincinnati Reds, is a regular on the celebrity pro-am circuit. Johnny is a congenital optimist on the golf course, a disciple of the school of positive thinking. We were partners in a match one day. Johnny hit into the trees and I was on the fairway. He came over to me and cheerfully declared, "Now, Bob, think positive. You're going to win this hole for us." I told him the only thing I was positive about was that I couldn't win that hole—and I didn't.

Drugs are very much on the scene in professional sports today, but when you think about it, golf is the only sport where the players aren't penalized for being on grass.

In my book some of the greatest celebrities in golf are the great blind players, like Charley Boswell of Birmingham, Alabama; Joe Lazaro of Waltham, Massachusetts; and Pat Brown of New Orleans. They are absolutely fabulous.

Charley Boswell wasn't always blind. He was a halfback on the University of Alabama Rose Bowl team of 1937 who lost his sight in World War II when he attempted to rescue a buddy from a tank just as a German shell exploded. He took up golf in 1946 and went on to win seventeen National

---

Martin and Lewis with a load at a National Golf Day exhibition in 1953 at the Cog Hill Golf Club in Chicago. National Golf Day was a big deal in those days, a genuine national competition for scratch and players and duffers sponsored by the PGA of America and Life *Magazine.*

I ASK WHATS BOROS GOING TO SHOOT?"

LET ME TELL YOU WHAT I SHOT

Second A
NA
GOLF DAY
PGA
LIFE
YOUR CHANCE
E CHAMP

and eleven International Blind Golfers' Championships. He once shot an 81, and in 1970 made a hole in one.

For the last eleven years he had held the Charley Boswell Celebrity Classic in Birmingham, which has raised over $800,000 for the Eye Foundation Hospital. I play in it every year. Jim Martin, an advertising and public relations man in Birmingham who also doubles as a sports writer, runs the tournament. Bear Bryant, the peerless Alabama coach, was an annual entry until he died and so are celebrities like Don Meredith, Neil Armstrong, Johnny Bench and Hubert Green.

It's really incredible to watch these blind golfers play. They have a coach who places the clubhead on line for them on each shot and tells them how far away the green is. Charley's longtime coach is a man named Bo Russell. On the green the golfers walk from the ball to the flagstick so they get a feel for distance, and then the coach sets the putter on line behind the ball. I once saw Boswell roll in a fifty-foot putt.

Boswell's celebrity tournament in Birmingham is held at the Point Aquarius Country Club, which has a lake on the 1st hole. A couple of years ago we had a foursome of Boswell, Bryant, myself and Harry Edwards a guy who had paid $5,000 to play with us. Harry hit his drive into the water. Bryant got over, and I just barely got over. Then Charley stepped up and knocked his drive 250 yards, far over the lake and right down the middle.

I always play 9 holes with Charley, and then do a show that night. When we reach the last hole I tell Charley, "It's time to go to the pocketbook. This hole's between us for $1.00." In 1982 I made a long putt for my par and Charley rapped in a 15-footer for a birdie.

One day Jim Martin asked Charley, "Do you know what Bob Hope actually looks like?" Charley thought for a moment and said, "Well, I remember his face from his early movies." He tells me I've got the worst swing he's ever heard.

Joe Lazaro, a doughty New Englander, is another of the giants of blind golf. Like Charley Boswell, Joe lost his sight during World War II. In 1942, while stationed in England, he met Edna ("Skip") Basnett, who would later become his wife. The last time he actually saw her was in 1942 before shipping out for North Africa with the 109th Combat Engineers. Later he landed on the beach at Salerno and fought under General Mark Clark in

---

Somewhere on the Victory Caravan during World War II. I can't recall where and the other three guys are no longer with us—Craig Wood on the left, Vic Ghezzi and Babe Ruth. You needed plenty of Red Cross volunteers around when the Babe was playing.

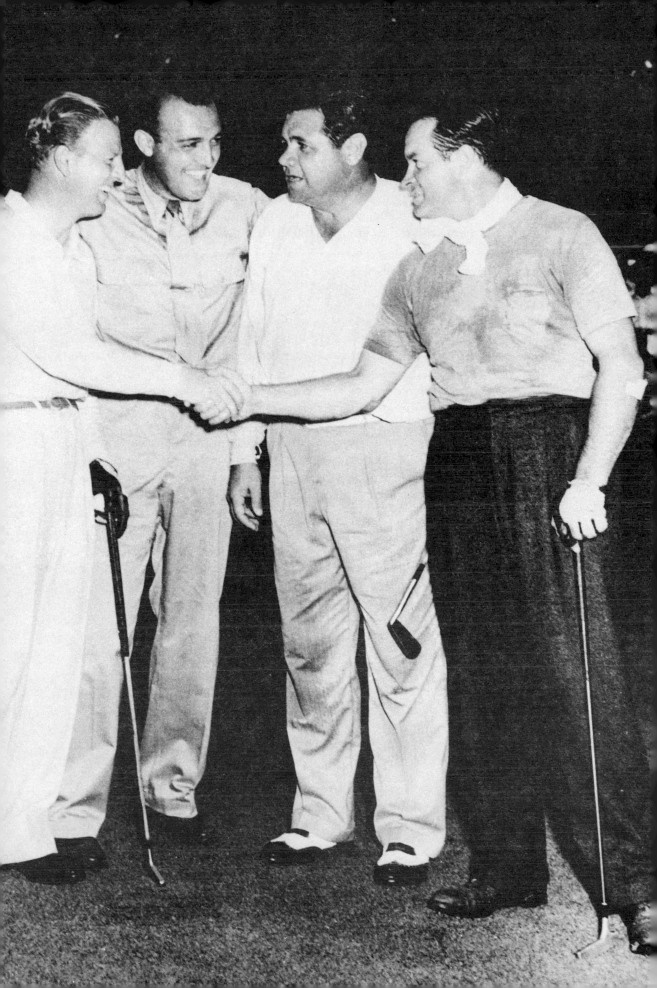

Italy before a land mine explosion on September 8, 1944, cost him his vision.

Joe took up golf for a spell in 1946, but really didn't get involved with it until 1950. Since 1962 he has won seven National Blind Golfers' Championships. Despite his handicap, Joe has always maintained a great sense of humor. One night at a golf dinner in Boston, where he and Sam Snead were honored, Joe challenged Snead to a match. The terms were that Snead could name the stakes and pick the course while Lazaro could select the time. Joe suggested they play at midnight.

I was playing with Joe one day at Clearwater, Florida, when he remarked, "You know, Bob, I'm glad I can't see the hazards on this course. They would scare the hell out of me."

Ronald Reagan is not particularly known for his golf. He favors other hobbies. But as a young actor in Hollywood he did play occasionally and now, while in the White House, he gets in one round a year at Walter Annenberg's private (meaning one-man) club in Palm Springs. We usually spend New Year's together, and last year when I went over to see him he was at the tag end of his press conference and I heard him say, "And I 1-putted 4 greens."

I've known Reagan for forty four years, but I never realized what a polished politician he had become—a real Irish politician—until one night in January 1983 when I heard him speaking on television. There was a man who truly loved his job. I like Ronald Reagan. He's smart, he's honest, and he's the only President who has ever called me "Sonny."

It didn't surprise me at all when I heard he wound up drinking beer at a bar in Boston, chatting with the regulars there. Reagan is comfortable with anyone. I also heard that on that same night the FBI was staking out a criminal in the next building and with the President there, and all the commotion, the sting was ruined.

I think the bar must have been full of Democrats. After Reagan finished his beer they locked the rest rooms. And the bartender must have been a comedian. When Reagan ordered a beer, the bartender looked at him and said, "Are you sure you're over twenty-one?"

Do you realize that Ronald Reagan may be the first President on Mount Rushmore sitting on a bar stool?

After the 1984 Summer Olympics, Reagan wanted to add the U.S. volleyball team to his Cabinet. He figured if they can't shove his programs down Congress' throat, nobody can.

Speaking of old actors, John Wayne was one of my best friends, but for some reason he never cared much for golf. Most of his pals and associates did. Grant Withers, a longtime crony of Duke, played regularly at Lakeside with Forrest Tucker, John Carroll and Herbert Yates. Yates was head of

Republic studios, and their boss. He loved to win. The actors would look the other way when Yates kicked his ball out of the rough. One day on the 18th tee, with all bets doubled, Yates whiffed his drive, and quickly looked around at the actors. Withers calmly said, "Take another one, Mr. Yates. We were thinking."

The wildest golfer I've ever seen—until Jerry Ford came along—was Babe Ruth. Tremendous power, but he knocked his shots all over the place. We were playing an exhibition at the Forest Hills Country Club in Bloomfield, New Jersey, when Ruth almost killed half a dozen people. The Red Cross ambulance sirens were making so much noise I couldn't concentrate on my backswing.

I'll never forget a round I played in Belgium with King Baudouin. The origin was a party in Hollywood at the home of Mervyn LeRoy. Baudouin, who was then Prince Baudouin, was the guest of honor. When it was time to leave, the prince came up to me and said, "If you're ever in Belgium, please look me up." Not long afterward he became King.

A couple of years later, to rest up after an eye operation, I traveled to Europe with my good friend Pardee Erdman, an excellent golfer who played in Pasadena and Pebble Beach. We played St. Andrews and Gleneagles in Scotland and then went to Monte Carlo to visit Princess Grace and Ranier at the palace. From there we flew to London and one night, as Pardee and I were sitting in our suite at the Savoy, I remembered Baudouin's invitation.

I reached for the phone and said, "Pardee, would you like to play with a King?" I called the king's equerry at the palace in Brussels and said, "This is Bob Hope. Would you tell the King that I'm in London and have golf clubs and will travel." He called back in about forty minutes and said there would be a car waiting for us at the airport in Brussels the next day.

The following morning we jumped on a plane for Brussels and were driven to the royal golf course, where we had lunch with the King. Then he introduced us to Jack Maurman, the Belgian Amateur champion. The match was set up: the King and I against Pardee and Maurman for a $10 nassau.

The King and I lost the front 9. On the 10th tee I told the King, "Let's give 'em a press. He said OK and then I said, "Let's make it a double press." I proceeded to take a double bogey on the 10th hole and on the way to the 11th tee, the King put his arm around me and said, "You must have a lot of money." This from a man who owned his own country.

Ruby Keeler and Paulette Goddard were the best golfers among the Hollywood actresses I played with during the 1940s, but no woman of that time could come close to matching the power of Babe Didrikson Zaharias. What a fantastic athlete she was. Babe was the star of the 1932 Summer Olympics in Los Angeles who later got into golf and won a total of eighty-two tournaments as an amateur and professional. She was an excellent bowler, tennis player, swimmer and diver, and could punt a football seventy-five yards. She was named Woman Athlete of the Year six times by the Associated Press, and in 1950 the A.P. picked her as Woman Athlete of the Half Century. In 1954, only fifteen months after cancer surgery, she won the U.S. Women's Open by twelve strokes.

In 1940 I was playing in an exhibition match at Cypress Point for the British War Relief Fund with Babe, Patty Berg and Pardee Erdman. It was Pardee and I against Patty and Babe. On the 18th hole I knocked in a long downhill putt to tie the match, so we went into an extra-hole sudden-death play-off. We halved the 1st hole and on the 2d, a par 5, Babe reached the front edge of the green with her second shot. Then she stepped up to the putt and made it, for an eagle 3. Match over.

Afterward I got a call from her husband, George Zaharias, who said simply, "You take care of my little girl." George was a professional wrestler, so I wasn't about to argue with him.

Babe liked to play to the audience. We did many exhibitions together. On a par-3 hole, if I hit first, she'd ask me, "What club did you use, Bob?" I'd say a 4-iron. In a loud voice that the gallery couldn't miss, she'd laugh and tell her caddie, "Give me an 8-iron."

One time Mickey Rooney and I had an exhibition with Babe at the Annandale Golf Club in Pasadena. George was there. Afterward we sat around in the clubhouse. George must have had a few too many beers, because he was walking around choking the members from behind, as they were sitting on their chairs, with his wrestling headlock. It was just a playful bear hug to George, but to the members it was life or death, and they didn't like it. They suggested he leave. Babe was sitting in front of the fireplace when George came over and said, "Come on, honey, we've got to go. They don't like the way I'm acting." Babe threw her beer into the fireplace. And then they left.

In their penetrating and candid biography of Babe called *Whatta Gal*, Bill Johnson and Nancy Williamson reminded us that on the September morning of 1956 when Babe died of cancer, President Eisenhower opened a press conference at the White House by declaring, "Ladies and gentlemen, I should like to take one minute to pay tribute to Mrs. Zaharias, Babe Didrikson. She was a woman who in her athletic career certainly won the admiration of every person in the United States, all sports people over the world. I think every one of us feels sad that finally she had to lose this last one of all her battles."

The last time I saw George Zaharias was at an LPGA tournament at Cleveland in 1976 that honored the Babe's memory. I did a show with the LPGA players in attendance. After it was over someone said to me, "There's a man out there who wants to see you. It's George Zaharias." He was sitting on the aisle in a wheelchair. George died a few years later.

I always did feel more comfortable over a pool table than on a putting green. Paulette Goddard thought it was funny, but then she's seen me putting in the regular style. We were appearing together on the Victory Caravan Exhibition in 1943.

In good company at the Los Angles Open in 1945: Linda Darnell, Babe Zaharias, Dot Kirby, Bing and Anne Baxter. Linda and Anne were young stars at the time, Babe and Dot two great pros. I have no idea why Crosby was in the picture.

Jack Benny was one of my favorite golf partners. The last time I played with him was at the O'Donnell course in Palm Springs, with Charlie Resnick and Danny Kaye. There was a lot of good-natured swearing over missed putts, to the point where the air was getting pretty blue. On the 8th tee there were three women from the Desert Inn sitting on the bench. Danny hit his drive out of bounds, looked up at the sky in despair and said, "Oh, shucks." Jack fell on the ground laughing. We had to drag him for two holes.

Speaking of celebrities, how about those American athletes in the 1984 Summer Olympics. America is a country where the Olympics and the divorce lawyers both have the same slogan—Go for the Gold. Everybody was worried about the traffic in Los Angeles before the Olympics started, but the only real traffic jam was Mary Decker and Zola Budd. Zola did for bare feet what Jerry Ford did for golf clubs.

Names are a problem for some celebrities. They meet so many people in so many different places. Once I was playing with Charley Farrell at O'Donnell when a guy shouted hello across the fairway to us and I said, "Hi, Sam." Farrell looked at me in surprise, and said, "How do you remember names like that? I have a terrible time."

I said that I was just fair at it, but got lucky once in a while. Charley shook his head. "I can't remember anyone's name," he said. "A guy walked up to me the other day and I said, 'Hello, I'm Charley Farrell.' The guy said, 'Yeah, Jackson Hole.' And I said, 'How are you, Mr. Hole?' "

Gerald Ford's gallery doesn't really come out to watch him play. They come to play chicken with his tee shots. He has a special kind of people in his gallery—the ones who like to sky dive and walk on hot coals.

I've played golf with nearly all the recent residents of the White House. I used to beat Eisenhower regularly. Mamie was a terrible putter. Ike's army colleague, General Omar Bradley, was addicted to golf. We played a lot together. I've got a par-3 hole at my North Hollywood home that measures about 150 yards. Bradley once hit his tee shot three inches away from the flag.

When Ike and Bradley were directing the Allied troops in Europe during World War II, Churchill could never understand their devotion to golf. Winston didn't care much for the game. When I was over in England doing shows for American servicemen during the war he saw me swing. He snickered and remarked, "Never before has anyone swung so hard for so little."

Four

Tips from the Top:
How Hogan
Honed My Game

I love playing with the pros. I've probably played more rounds with the stars of the PGA Tour than any amateur alive. It started back in the 1930s, when Ben Hogan, Sam Snead, Byron Nelson and Jimmy Demaret were in the early stages of their careers. After all, golf is my real profession. Entertainment is just a sideline. I tell jokes to pay my greens fees.

If I'd have had to pay the pros for all the lessons they've given me over the years I'd be out walking the streets with a tin cup. The boys have really been great with me. Most of their advice is handed out on the practice tee, before we go off in a pro-am. In 1983 at Westchester I was hitting practice balls next to Jerry Pate. Jerry watched me for a minute or two. Then he came over and said, "You're breaking your left arm at impact, instead of extending it out like this." He showed me how, in that classical Pate swing. I started hitting the ball solidly right away, and had a good round.

Sometimes it's on the course, like during the Westchester pro-am in 1982. Tom Watson noticed that my putting was awful. I was taking the club back too far, cutting across the ball and decelerating at the moment of impact. You can't do many more things wrong on the putting green. Watson shortened my backswing with the putter and emphasized a popping motion through the ball, the same way he putts. All this, mind you, in front of four thousand people while we were actually playing the round. It takes a lot of patience to put up with my game under those conditions.

One of my all-time favorites has to be Arnold Palmer. No golfer has ever electrified the galleries like Arnie. I got to know him well, not only as a five-time winner of the Desert Classic but also through our work together in television and the movies. He's had a class act, right from the start.

The first time I saw Arnold was in the mid-1950s, shortly after he had turned professional. He had won the U.S. Amateur in 1954, but that didn't have much impact upon the general public. I was playing with Gene Littler in the pro-am of the Los Angeles Open when I spotted this muscular guy with the wide shoulders over in an adjoining fairway. I asked Littler who he was and Gene replied, "That's Arnold Palmer. He's going to be a great player. When he hits that ball the earth shakes."

Later that day I watched him play a couple of holes, and Littler was right. The ground did shake. After his round I was introduced to him, and as we were standing there chatting I had the feeling I was looking at a blacksmith. The man just radiated raw power.

Arnold went on to win the Masters in 1958 and 1960, and when he won the U.S. Open in 1960 at Denver, with a 65 on the last round, he became a walking legend. I had him on my TV show a couple of times, and he was good. In one skit I asked him if he'd mind working on my game. Arnold smiled that natural Latrobe, Pennsylvania, smile and said, "I've already seen your game. I think you should take up tennis."

Shortly after that I signed to do a picture entitled *Call Me Bwana,* an African adventure film that was to be shot in Kenya. I wanted Arnold to have a role, so in the fall of 1961 I flew up to the Seattle Open, where he was playing, to talk with him about it.

Palmer didn't show much enthusiasm for traveling to Kenya. I told him to sit tight, that the political situation in Kenya might be such that we couldn't work there. When we decided to shoot the picture in England, Arnold agreed.

The character I played was Matt Merriwether, a cowardly explorer who was constantly pursued by Anita Ekberg and Edie Adams. It was one of my most enjoyable roles. Arnold made his film debut in the scene where I was having breakfast alone in my tent. As I examined my egg cup I noticed something hard and round. Arnold poked his head through the slat with the line "Anybody seen my ball in here?"

There was a golf sequence where Arnold and I hit balls in the midst of what was meant to be a jungle clearing. We'd practice during a break in the shooting and then Arnold would put on a clinic for the crew.

Arnold had just won his second straight British Open. There were between fifty and sixty newspaper guys on the scene, who had come to see Palmer. Half the time the director would line them up—he thought they were extras. One day Arnold staged a little show for the writers. There was a big rock out about 240 yards from the tee. Arnold would take a 1-iron and say, "Which side do you want the shot on?" Left side—he hit it. Right side—same thing. It was awesome.

We had a weekend break in the schedule and on Saturday I wanted to take Arnold over to play Dendham, a very proper old English course. The club captain heard about it. He called me and said, "We have a tournament on Saturday and I wouldn't take Palmer out here if I were you."

What he meant was that it would be inconvenient for us to get around the course, but it didn't sound that way. It was probably the first time Arnold had been denied access to a golf course anywhere.

I told Arnold not to worry. English clubs are very exclusive. I played Royal Foxshire and they made me wear a suit and tie . . . in the shower. You can't get a starting time on Sunday unless you've been knighted.

I played on the winning team with Arnold in a pro-am at Phoenix, shooting a 75 on my own ball with a 35 on the front 9. I was on the putting green before the round when the late Bo Wininger, a wonderful guy, came over to watch me. "All left arm," he said. "Putting's all in the left arm." That day I holed everything I looked at. Arnold, I'm sure, was astounded.

On the 16th hole I told him, "Remember that old gag about wearing Arnold Palmer shirts and using Arnold Palmer shirts and using Arnold Palmer balls and playing like Betsy Palmer? Well, today I'm using Arnold Palmer clubs. They play better than I do."

Perfect lie for Arnold. Mike Douglas and Doug Sanders think it's funny as Palmer gets a free lift during an exhibition benefit for the Heart Association of Southeastern Pennsylvania at the Aronimink Golf Club, suburban Philadelphia, in 1966.

I'm teaching Arnold Palmer how to play with a bent shaft. Actually I hit some of my best shots with this club—and never slice.

Arnold Palmer trying to teach his swing to a skeptical pupil during the filming of Call Me Bwana in 1963. Arnold had a part in the movie and hit golf shots for us during breaks in the shooting.

Arnold enjoyed appearing on my television show in the 1960s. When you're young, you take chances. The public idolized him. He was golf's All-American boy. Now some people call him the "Old Man of Golf," but that's ridiculous. He can still play with the best of them. Just the other day he shot an eagle. Unfortunately he was in his plane at the time.

A few years ago Arnold went on a fitness program. He started jogging, and gave up smoking. And he looks great. He coughs only when his opponent is putting.

I've always thought Arnold's wife Winnie was a great influence on him. Through his good days and bad, Winnie was there, in the gallery. No tour wife was ever more knowledgeable in golf matters than Winnie. Arnold had a bad putting round one day in Phoenix and afterward Winnie called him off the practice green. "You know what you were doing out there, don't you?" she said. "You were raising your head just a fraction before your stroke was completed."

Arnold has been golf's most intrepid pilot. He has owned his own jet for years, often taking over the controls himself. This can get dangerous. On one flight he thought he was in a golf cart and stepped out at forty thousand feet.

In the 1961 Los Angeles Open, at Rancho Park, Arnold hit four of the longest drives of his life. Unfortunately they were all on the 9th hole—out of bounds. Arnold wasn't partial. He hit two to the left and two to the right. Seven fans in his Army were so dismayed they threw themselves off George Archer.

The next year they installed a plaque where Arnold had taken those twelve strokes. He took part in the dedication with his usual gracious humor. Palmer returned in 1963 to win the tournament with a 66 on the final round that included birdies on the last 2 holes.

In 1966 he won again at Rancho with a 62 in the third round and came back the next year to win it by five strokes. Arnold was just as invulnerable in L.A. as he was in Palm Springs. He's always played well in California. And they love him everywhere. There were two things that made golf appealing to the average man . . . Arnold Palmer and the invention of the mulligan.

Arnold has been an idol of millions for three decades. He has been a wonderful influence on young people, a symbol of exemplary sportsmanship in victory or defeat. His fame and charisma are legendary. When Arnie was charging, an entire nation rooted for him. Arnie's Army doesn't just consist of his golf fans. It includes countless Americans who recognize that his character, stability and just plain niceness will be emulated by generations to come. He is truly a man for all seasons.

Jack Nicklaus has won more major championships (nineteen at last count) than anyone in golf history, but to me he has made an equally indelible

It couldn't have been that bad. Jack Nicklaus gives one of my gags the ho-hum reaction during an exhibition in 1973 at the Kings Island course in Cincinnati. Nicklaus designed the course, which now holds the LPGA Championship each year.

The top pros don't sink every putt. And when they miss 'em, it hurts. Ask Jack Nicklaus.

impression upon the game in many other ways. His career has been embellished with dignity, impeccable conduct, sportsmanship, a rare ability to mesh golf in with his business interests and his family and, surely not to be overlooked, his contributions to golf through his course architecture.

I've played in nearly every pro-am at the Memorial, the tournament Jack founded at Muirfield Village in Dublin, Ohio, in 1976. It was a particularly memorable experience for me in 1983. It was the week of my eightieth birthday and on the first tee they rolled out a huge cake. I have never seen galleries that large anywhere. They were massive, lining both sides of the fairway on every hole. On each tee the spectators broke out in a spontaneous rendition of "Happy Birthday."

That was nice, of course, but how much can I take? I mean, eighty is when you order a steak and the headwaiter puts it through the blender. Or when you wake up as many times during the night as Burt Reynolds, but not for the same reason. When George Burns turned eighty he said, "I can do all the things today I did at eighteen . . . which tells you how pathetic I was at eighteen."

But it was a great day, even though Jack's course is so difficult. I had a 9 on the 1st hole before I got it out of the ball washer. In recent years Jack has modified the course a little. When Muirfield Village first opened even the pros had trouble. Ed Sneed told him, "Jack, you've built a house without any windows." Meaning that there was no escape. I was playing in the pro-am with Sam Snead one year when his second shot on the par-5 15th hole, a perfect shot right down the middle of the fairway, rolled into a creek. Sam was fuming. "What kind of a course have you got here?" he asked Nicklaus. "Some of those holes weren't meant to be." Jack softened it up a little over the years and today it's a fair and beautiful course, a lasting testimonial to the man who built it.

Jack won the Desert Classic in 1963, the tournament in which he started using Angie Argea as his permanent caddie. It was a partnership that lasted nearly twenty years. Angie became quite a wit. In an exhibition with Jack I hit a particularly good shot. I turned to Angie and asked him, "How do you like the way my hips follow through?" In that deadpan way of his, he said, "Swell, but what do you want me to find, the ball or your girdle?"

Nan, Jack's only daughter, has a volleyball scholarship at the University of Georgia. I've always felt like sort of a godfather to Nan, and here's why:

In 1965 I played a charity exhibition at the Scioto Country Club in Columbus with Jack. Afterward my brother Fred and I went to the Nicklaus home for dinner. Barbara had served the salad and suddenly she disappeared. "It's time, Jack," she said. She left for the hospital to deliver Nan. Fred and I wound up grilling the steaks.

I once saw Nicklaus drive the green on the 7th hole at Scioto, a hole that measures 371 yards with a slight dogleg. He drove the green and sank the putt for an eagle. I said, "How come I can't hit the ball like that?" You know what he came back with—a little surprising from Nicklaus? "You'd get more distance if you took the head covers off your woods." Not bad.

What amazes me is the power that Jack can generate from those small hands. One day I was playing at Scioto with Charlie Nicklaus, Jack's dad, and a couple of other guys. For some reason I didn't have a glove in my bag. Charlie said, "Use one of Jack's," and he went to his locker and got one for me. I couldn't get my hand into it. Jack has smaller hands than I do.

Jack gave me one of the most valuable instant lessons I've ever received. I had been a miserable bunker player for a long time. We were playing an exhibition somewhere, I forget where it was. After watching me flounder around in the traps for the first few holes, Jack went into a bunker with me and showed me how to get out. "Keep the left shoulder down," he said. I started hitting down and through the ball, instead of trying to scoop it out. I've always been grateful to Jack for that.

Do you know that I almost got him retired? What a snafu that was. In the fall of 1979 I called Jack to remind him that I'd sure like to have him in the Classic the following January. Jack wasn't feeling too good about his game at that time. He had his worst year in 1979 and I could tell he was really down.

He said he was cutting back his schedule in 1980 and "may not play in any West Coast tournaments." We must have had a bad connection. I could have sworn he said "may not play in any tournaments." Retire, for the year at least. Well, the next day I flew to Boston for a show and mentioned that to one of the writers there. It made all the wire services and caused a real flap. I called Jack to apologize for my misinterpretation.

Nicklaus not only did not retire in 1980, he came back to win the U.S. Open and the PGA Championship.

Few golfers have ever changed their image more dramatically than Nicklaus. When he first burst into the public eye he was chubby, wore a bristling crewcut and dressed like someone who got his apparel in a close-out sale. I was there, at Rancho Park, when Jack played his first professional tournament, the 1962 Los Angeles Open. His check was for $33.33.

In 1969 Nicklaus decided to alter his appearance. He went on a diet and lost thirty pounds. He let his hair grow. He signed with Hart Schafner

---

Swinging in top form for the master, Ben Hogan. I took a number of lessons from Ben in the early 1950s, which of course helped my game immeasurably, and I got to know him well. Under that stern facade was, at least on some occasions, a warm nature. And what a player!

Jimmy Demaret and Ben Hogan putting their weight on me while the lovely Dagmar tries to give us all a lift. Jimmy and Ben, totally opposite in temperament and attitude, were close friends who teamed together to win many a four-ball tournament in the early days of the tour.

Taking an informal lesson from Ben Hogan. Ben is having a little fun here, and he did have his moments like that, but primarily he was a very serious student of the game. He was one of the finest teachers I've ever had. The guy on the right must have been from the IRS, checking our winnings.

The microphones outnumber the golfers as Sam Snead and Bing match dialogues. That's Lew Worsham in the middle and Claude Harmon on the right.

Marx. He became more outgoing, more at ease with the public and the press. The galleries grew to love him, and he returned that warmth. I watched this all happen, year after year. The Nicklaus metamorphosis took place right in front of my eyes.

Developing a new image with the public is harder than sainthood. Saints don't have to give autographs. They just have to perform miracles, and Nicklaus does that every time he swings a golf club.

I was thinking about Ben Hogan recently, remembering what a great teacher he was. I spent many hours with Ben on the golf course and on the practice tee. On the course he was an absolute perfectionist, and he carried a good share of that quality into his everyday life.

We played once in the Crosby at Rancho Santa Fe before the war. The next time I saw him was in 1942, in a war relief exhibition at Topeka, Kansas. He was a much better golfer by this time. Not long after that we were together again for a round in Dallas. On 2 par-4 holes, each about 380 yards, Hogan was right in front of the green with his drive. The fairways were hard and dry, that's true, but that is really swatting the ball.

We continued to play here and there for the next several years. In 1949 he had that terrible accident, when a bus hit the car he was driving in a head-on collision. He came back to win two straight U.S. Opens and then one day I read where he had become the pro at Tamarisk, in Palm Springs. Here was my chance to tap him for a few lessons.

Hogan told me he did his teaching in the mornings. "That's no good for you," he said. "I know you sleep late every morning."

"Well, I want you to show me something. I'll get up if you'll work with me."

"OK, we'll start tomorrow morning at 9."

I was a 6-handicap at the time but I had trouble playing to it. Hogan did wonders for me. He firmed up my grip and extended my takeaway and soon I was tagging the tee shots 230 to 240 yards. He still didn't think I took the game seriously enough. You know Ben.

We started playing for $10 nassaus, Ben from the back tees. After he had beaten me one day we were sitting in the clubhouse, sipping iced teas. Tamarisk is an excellent course, with just about the same yardage as Augusta National, where Hogan won the Masters in 1951 and 1953.

"This is a nice golf course," he said, referring to Tamarisk. "A nice 68 par."

I looked at him and said, "What? How do you figure that?"

"Well, I figure to get home on the par 5s in two. I'll make a bogey here, but I'll make a birdie there. It comes to 68."

"To me it's a 72 par, so if you feel that way, give me another four shots." Hogan said no way, but I finally talked him into it.

The next day I shot 75 and broke even with him. I considered it an artistic triumph.

That period of time, during the early 1950s, was the best stretch of golf I've ever played. My handicap at Lakeside got down to 4, although I had to struggle hard to play to it. I invited Hogan up to play with me at Lakeside. He accepted. The word got around and everyone was looking forward to his arrival.

Just before he showed up I looked up Brandon Hurst, the Lakeside handicap chairman, in the grill room. "I need two more shots for Hogan," I told him. "You know I'm having a tough time with that 4. Switch me to a 6, Brandy, I need your help." Brandy called me a thief, but he did it.

So Hogan comes and he says, "I'll give you two shots a side." I just smiled. "Sorry, Ben," I told him, "you have to give me three a side now. I'm a 6." We argued over that for a while, but I showed him the card that Brandy Hurst had signed and I got my 6 strokes.

On the 9th hole I hit my second shot over the green and chipped back for a 4. I was 1 under par at the turn and 1 up on Hogan. As we walked to the 10th tee he gave me another lesson.

On the back 9 I shot 40, which gave me 74 for the day against Hogan's 69. He was always a hard man to beat.

I never did take another lesson from him, but I knew he kept track of my golf and shortly after I went to the Greenbrier Resort in White Sulphur Springs, West Virginia, for a pro–am. Hogan was there. My handicap was back to 6, but Stuart Symington, who was running the tournament, said, "I'll give you a 9." I said fine.

My partner the first round was Shelley Mayfield, a good player. Shelley shot a 71. So did I, on my own ball. It was the best round of golf I've ever played, if you don't count a 66 at O'Donnell, a short course in Palm Springs. I was ecstatic.

When I came in, there was Hogan, waiting for me. "What did you have?" he asked me. I could hardly wait to tell him. "I shot 71," I said proudly. He looked at me kind of funny.

"You mean net, with your handicap."

"No, I mean I shot a natural 71."

"You're kidding. Bob, that's wonderful. I'm proud of you."

I didn't see Ben for a few years after that. Then one night they had a big dinner in Fort Worth for Byron Nelson on the eve of the Byron Nelson Classic. I was sitting at the head table, along with Hogan, Cary Middlecoff, Jimmy Demaret, some others and, of course, Byron. Hogan looked over at me and said, "I want to talk to you about your golf swing."

He must have been watching me on television. So he got me out in the lobby and gave me a lesson right there. The people walking by couldn't believe it. Hogan just doesn't do that sort of thing. I thought it was wonderful.

Keeping score, in my fashion, with Lee Trevino at the Desert Classic. Lee, an old favorite with the Palm Springs crowd, made a smooth transition to the NBC microphones.

You can't ever think of Hogan without thinking of Sam Snead, because they were so closely related in the public's mind. The two greatest players of their day. They weren't exactly pals, but their rivalry in the postwar years kept golf on the front sports pages. And they were vastly different, in every way.

Snead, colorful and charismatic, had the mountaineer's natural suspicion of strangers. It took a while for us to become friends, but I always found him a delightful companion on the golf course and also a great storyteller. His frugality was legend. You've heard all the stories about how he had his money buried in his backyard.

Sam gave me lots of advice, but I didn't take it. I figured banks were safer than tin cans. I once visited Sam at his home and would you believe . . . his backyard was six feet lower than his house.

Snead's manager for years was Fred Corcoran, one of golf's great public relations men. Fred got a lot of press for Sam, and he was always pressuring him to be nice to the writers. When Snead was playing in a New York–area tournament, Corcoran took out a midtown suite for him and suggested he invite the writers up for a drink. Bill Corum, Dan Parker, Frank Graham . . . they all came. Sam had ordered the liquor from room service. The next day Snead approached Corcoran and said, "Do you know that those writers drank a whole pint of scotch?"

One of golf's liveliest events in the 1950s was the Tournament of Champions, held in May at the Desert Inn at Las Vegas. The calcuttas were unbelievable. I was the chief auctioneer a couple of times and once the bidding got a little slow. Some guy bid $5,000 on Tommy Bolt. "Come on," I told him. "You could lose that much on the way to the men's room."

Snead was a popular attraction at Vegas. For two years Morrie Kleinman and I bought him for about $19,000 and Sam bombed out in the first round. Those were the days when Gene Littler had a lock on that tournament—three straight. Frankie Laine had him each time and wound up building a Gene Littler Room in his house with the profits.

If I sound like an old-timer, dwelling on guys like Hogan and Snead, don't forget that I've been playing golf so long I wash my golf balls with epsom salts. Just the other day I was asking Snead if he had lost any distance off the tee. He said, "I think so. I swing just as hard, but I walk slower and get to the ball quicker."

Sam and I once collaborated on a celebrity golf film series that was shot at Lakeside. He came out about a dozen times for the tapings and got to know the club's staff pretty well. Norm Blackburn produced the show, which we're going to syndicate in Japan soon. At seventy-plus Sam's still a big name in golf.

Everyone's signed their John Henry to this shot of our group at the Bryon Nelson Classic in 1977. Tom Watson had just won his first Masters, and two months later would beat Jack Nicklaus in that great duel in the British Open at Turnberry. It was Jerry Ford's first year out of the White House.

Not many people know this, but I discovered George Bayer. He was knocking around in Nevada, playing in local pro tournaments, when I spotted him one day at Incline Village. I had never seen anybody hit a ball like that. He said he had played football for the Washington Redskins. The guy was huge even by NFL standards.

I told him to call me the next day, and he did. Harry Cooper, who was then the pro at Lakeside, had played a lot of golf with Jimmy Thomson, the great long hitter of his day. I wanted Harry to take a look at this Bayer character. We played 9 holes. George was knocking them out of sight and Harry was shaking his head in awe.

Just as we came in I got a call from Bus Ham of the Washington *Post*, who was putting on a celebrity tournament the following week. He was calling to confirm my appearance in the tournament. I said I'd be there, but he should also invite this Bayer guy. I put Harry Cooper on the phone with Bus. "I've played golf all over the world," Harry said, "and I've never seen anybody hit a ball that far." Bayer was invited.

They paired him with Snead, of all people. On the first hole Sam, who did not watch Bayer drive, walked up to Bayer's ball way out on the fairway and said, "Is this your second shot, boy?" Bayer replied, "No, this is my drive." George must have been forty or fifty yards out beyond Sam's ball. When the realization set in, Snead looked at Bayer in that squinty way of his and asked him, "Where are you from, son?"

On the next hole Porky Oliver, playing in the group ahead of Snead and Bayer, hit his second shot and walked up the fairway when a ball came bounding past him. Porky spun around to find out what the hell was going on. He saw this moose standing on the tee holding up both hands, as if in apology. Porky was a hefty hitter himself.

Well, the word got around fast and within a couple of days Toney Penna signed him for MacGregor. George had a successful career in golf, first as a tour player and later as a club professional. And he could hit it past anyone.

Lee Trevino is one of my favorite golfing characters. He's the greatest Mexican since Dolores Del Rio. And how he loves to talk. He makes Joan Rivers sound like Calvin Coolidge. Lee has done very well financially with those television commercials. Why not, he's got you coming and going. If his enchiladas backfire he sells you some aspirin.

Lee's career nearly ended when he was struck by lightning during the Western Open in 1975, which caused him a lot of serious back problems. I love Lee's line: "I should have been carrying a 1-iron that day. Even God can't hit a 1-iron." Personally, if I'm on the course and lightning starts, I get inside fast. If God wants to play through, let him.

Trevino is so quick with the one-liners that sometimes his spontaneous humor obscures his immense ability. But to me he's one of the finest shotmakers of all time. When you win two U.S. Opens, two British Opens and two PGA Championships you don't do it with quips.

Wasn't he fabulous in winning the 1984 PGA? I watched it on TV and it was great. Lee had to wait ten years since his previous major championship. Ten years of waiting and commenting and watching the swings of other players, picking out the good points. That PGA was a big day in his life.

But the jokes are still part of his image. He was married in 1983 to a woman named Claudia, which also happened to be the name of his previous wife. "Couldn't have worked out better," Lee said, "I didn't even have to change the names on the towels."

One of the first members of Tom Watson's fan club was my wife Dolores. She fell in love with Tom when he first came out on the tour in 1971, a carbon copy of Huck Finn with those freckles and shy smile. He had such a boyish look about him that he was the only pro whose putter had training wheels.

Like most top pros, Tom had to learn how to lose before he learned how to win. He blew a tournament in Hawaii, another one at Hilton Head and yet another at Sawgrass. Then he let the 1974 U.S. Open slip through his hands with that last-round 79 at Winged Foot.

But Tom got tough, and with that toughness came his great victories. He reminds me of Hogan in the way he can repair his game during a tournament. A few years ago I played with him in the pro-am of the Los Angeles Open. He was having a terrible time, driving into the rough and pushing his iron shots right off the green. I felt sorry for him.

On the back 9 he began working on his swing, walking down the fairways practicing his follow-through, clearing his left side out of the way. I watched him, but said nothing. Tom won that tournament, in an exciting play-off with Johnny Miller.

I'd rank Tom with the all-time greats in putting ability and self-assurance. When you have those kind of trophies on your mantle (five in the British Open alone) you can afford a little cockiness, believe me.

The first tip-off I got on Watson's future greatness came from Arnold Palmer, years ago. Palmer had played an exhibition with Watson in Kansas City when Tom was the fourteen-year-old Missouri Amateur champion. I saw Arnold a few weeks later and he told me, "Bob, you won't believe this kid I played with. He is going to be super." Arnold, as usual, was right on the money.

In the last few years I've played quite a bit with the women pros. Can't beat that duty. Jan Stephenson is an example of the eye-catching talent currently on the LPGA Tour. I watched Jan's stroke and almost suffered one myself. I wanted to play with her, but couldn't get a note from my doctor. I asked her how she likes my game and she said, "Well, it's OK, but I still prefer golf."

I was with JoAnne Carner in the pro-am of the 1983 Dinah Shore tournament. JoAnne's a marvelous player. I don't know how she generates all that power with such a short backswing. On one hole she had a 180-yard shot to the green and took out a 9-iron. I said, "A 9-iron?" Replied JoAnne, "It's against the wind."

Dinah is the hostess at the biggest tournament in women's golf, held at Mission Hills in Rancho Mirage, California, which is in the Greater Palm Springs area. The Colgate people started it in 1972, thanks largely to the efforts of David Foster, who was then the company's chief executive officer. Nabisco took it over ten years later. Dinah plays in the pro-am every year. She takes what she calls her "crash course" in golf for about two weeks preceding the tournament. Dinah, by the way, was on my first TV show. Of course she was just a child at the time. She had to have a chaperone before she could blow a kiss.

One year Dinah let me play in the tournament proper. I was leading after 5 holes. Then my wig fell off and they discovered I wasn't Pat Bradley.

As you can obviously tell, I love the pros and appreciate all the lessons and all the help they've given me. Unfortunately it doesn't seem to have done much good. I still play Bermuda Dunes like the Bermuda Triangle.

Agony in motion. Tom Watson anguishes over one that didn't fall. Watson expects to make everything on the greens. So do I, providing they give me a mulligan or two.

Five

Ike

In 1943 I was doing a series of shows for U.S. servicemen in North Africa. Our group was quartered at the Aletti Hotel in Algiers. Quentin Reynolds, Bruce Cabot and H. R. Knickerbocker were also there. Quent had come across a large supply of scotch, and we celebrated vigorously far into the night.

The next morning I went over to the Red Cross building with Hal Bloch and Frances Langford to start rehearsing a radio broadcast. Tony Romano was already there. We had just begun work when a Colonel Hill walked in. "Could I talk to you for a minute?" he asked. I replied, "You can see me anytime, but not today. We've got a show to do here tonight."

The colonel stood there a few moments and then he said, "I'm General Eisenhower's aide. The general would like to see you right away." That was the end of the rehearsal.

I had never met Eisenhower. I told the gang, "Take a break," and followed the colonel. Ike was seated behind a desk in his command post, studying some maps. He got up quickly, walked over to extend his hand. His first words to me were "How's your golf?"

That was the beginning of a beautiful friendship that endured for over a quarter of a century. Ike and I traveled a lot of miles together, many of them on the golf course, and we often mentioned how it all got started that day back in Algiers.

As I was about to leave Ike's office, he gave our group signed pictures of himself, which the gang gobbled up, and then said to me, "I understand you've been through some bombings." I said, "Yes, a couple, and they're not for me. They affect my backswing."

"Relax," Ike said, "we haven't had any bombing here for some time. You'll get a nice rest tonight."

That night about 4 A.M. all hell broke loose. We ran down to the wine cellar they were using for an air raid shelter. They were shooting antiaircraft guns from the top of the hotel. You never heard such a rattle. The whole scene was terrifying. I kept thinking that if the building collapses, it comes down right on top of us.

Just before leaving the next day, I sent a little note down to Eisenhower that read, "Thanks for the rest."

By the time Ike was elected President in 1952, his devotion to golf had become legendary. No administration ever had more sun-tanned Secret Service men. You could always find his farm at Gettysburg because it was the one completely surrounded by divots. Ike's neighbors didn't know he had moved in until Mamie knocked at their door and asked to borrow a cup of golf balls.

Ike loved the Augusta National Golf Club. He visited there for the first time in April of 1948, staying eleven days, and later he became a dues-paying member. Ike generally played the course in the low 90s, occasionally

That's Ike, bursting out of the Fairbanks Golf and Country Club in Alaska. The kid on the left seems interested—he must have been waiting for me. I don't know where I was at the moment, probably still back in the locker room.

breaking into the 80s, and the club never had a more devoted member. While in the White House he made twenty-nine trips to stay and play at Augusta National.

On May 8, 1953, I spoke at the White House Correspondents Dinner. Ike, of course, was there. I kidded him about his golf, about all those divots on the White House lawn. Not to mention the divots he'd been tearing up down in Augusta. I guess that's what the Republicans meant when they said they'd break up the Solid South.

Then I gave them the caddie joke that goes like this:

Ike was playing down at Augusta National the other day and he hit a bad shot. His caddie remarked, "You certainly goofed that one, mister." The other caddie in the group scolded him. He said, "You don't talk that way, LeRoy. That's the President of the United States!"

On the next hole Ike hit one out of bounds. The chastized caddie said, "You certainly freed that one, Mr. Lincoln."

Ike was a golfer to warm every weekender's heart, playing with gusto and determination. He fumed over his bad shots and exulted over his good ones, scrapping for every dollar on the line.

When Ike was President I played with him at Burning Tree, against General Omar Bradley and Senator Stuart Symington. On the 1st tee we discussed wagers. "Well," Ike said with that infectious smile, "I just loaned Bolivia $2 million. I'll play for a dollar nassau."

I played terribly and we lost. The next day I teamed with Senator Prescott Bush against Ike and General Bradley. I was back on my game and shot 75. I beat Ike for $4.00 and I'll never forget the sour look on his face when he pulled out his money clip and paid off. He looked me in the eye and grumbled, "Why didn't you play this well yesterday?" He wasn't laughing, either.

Another course Ike liked to play was Eldorado, in Palm Springs. During his two terms as President he often came out to the desert during the winter, and never failed to get in a round or two. Eldorado has grapefruit trees in the rough, where Ike spent a lot of his time, and he was always picking up grapefruits while looking for his ball. One day he got really exasperated and said, "When I get back to the White House, if anyone serves me grapefruit they're fired!"

One of Ike's strongest rivals for the 1952 Republican presidential nomination was Robert Taft, who was also a dedicated golfer. Ike won the nomination, and shortly after he and Taft had a reconciliation round of golf at Burning Tree. The next day a friend of mine was in the Senate gallery, with his two sons. Down on the floor, engaged in earnest conversation with a couple of other senators, was Robert Taft.

My friend told his sons, "Look, boys, there's Robert Taft, one of the great Americans of all time. He's probably discussing some of the most

In a nostalgic reunion from the North African campaign of 1943, Ike greets Frances Langford at the Desert Classic. Dolores and I both got a kick out of that emotional meeting.

Ike and slender Billy Casper at the Desert Classic in 1966. Billy, on his exotic diet of buffalo meat and other assorted delicacies at the time, was the defending champion. Later that year he beat Arnold Palmer in a play-off for the U.S. Open.

Here's one of my favorite mementos of Ike, at the Desert Classic in 1966. Ike was the only person I know who fought two world wars with an overlap grip.

Arnold Palmer shares a moment with Ike at the Desert Classic while Cary Middlecoff, on cue, awaits with his NBC microphone. Arnold, the most popular golfer ever to play in Palm Springs, is a five-time Classic winner and a champion in every way. That's Ernie Dunlevie, one of the key guys of the Classic, in the background.

important issues of the world with those men, issues that will affect all of our lives."

At that moment Taft pushed the men aside and went into his golf swing.

Ike liked to tell the story about two golfers in front of the green. One lay eight, the other nine. The one who had taken nine strokes said, "It's your hole. My short game is lousy."

When I got involved with the Desert Classic in 1965 Ike became an important part of the tournament. He really enjoyed watching the competition, and he always participated in the presentation ceremonies. In 1965 Billy Casper made a four-foot birdie putt on the final hold at Bermuda Dunes to beat Arnold Palmer by a stroke. At the awards program Ike turned to Billy and said, "That was a real knee-knocker." Will Grimsley of the Associated Press picked it up and it made every paper in the country the next morning.

In 1968, Ike's last year at the Classic, we arranged a little surprise for him. He was sitting in the bleachers with Mamie behind the 18th green at Bermuda Dunes. Over on the 1st fairway, unknown to Ike, General Bill Yancey, who was then the tournament's executive secretary, was assembling a combination of army, navy and air force bands.

The moment that play was completed, the bands moved into position on the 18th fairway and marched in unison toward Ike, playing all of his favorite songs. Ike was deeply moved. Mamie told me, "That's the first time in years I've seen tears come into his eyes."

Ironically, Palmer and Deane Beman, later to become commissioner of the PGA Tour, had tied after 90 holes and had to go into a sudden-death play-off while the bands were playing. The play-off started on 14. Yancey was worried that the play-off might get to 18 before the bands were through playing. Arnold took care of that by closing it out on 16.

Ike played quite a bit of golf with Arnold at Augusta National, where Palmer had won the Masters four times. They became close friends. Ike, Mamie and Winnie Palmer cooked up a little surprise for Arnold on his thirty-seventh birthday, September 10, 1966. Arnold was reading in the den of the Palmer home in Latrobe, Pennsylvania, when the doorbell rang. "Arn, why don't you see who that can be?" asked Winnie. When Arnold opened the door, there was Ike, that big smile spreading across his face. "Happy birthday, pro," he said. "Could you put up with another guest?" Mamie joined them a couple of hours later.

The birthday gift Ike presented to Palmer that day was one of his paintings, a rural scene in Pennsylvania. Ike loved to paint. I always kidded him that he preferred painting to golf because it required fewer strokes.

I don't suppose anyone has ever done more to popularize golf than Ike. He was truly hooked on the game. It was no coincidence that golf enjoyed

Ike goes for a one-liner during the awards ceremonies at the Classic. I wish I could remember the joke.

a widespread burst of growth during Ike's years as President. He brought a sort of White House sanction to the game, a conviction of belief that it could be vastly enjoyed by middle-aged men with middle-age handicaps.

Golf Digest magazine got a tremendous promotion when it dispersed thousands of circular badges with Ike's picture and the words DON'T ASK WHAT I SHOT. The truth was that Ike played a perfectly respectable game. And no one every enjoyed it more. During his White House years there was a rumor going around that the new dollar bill would have Ben Hogan's picture on it.

It was always an honor to play with Ike. Playing golf with America's Presidents is a great denominator. How a President acts in a sand trap is a pretty good barometer of how he would respond if the hot line suddenly lit up—and some of his language proved it.

Of all the golf Ike played around the world, I believe many of his happiest rounds were with Freeman Gosden, the "Amos" of "Amos 'n' Andy," after he left the White House and retired to Palm Springs. Ike lived on the 11th fairway at Eldorado in those years. He and Freeman were great pals. Freeman would call Ike in the morning and say, "Can you play today, Mr. President?" and Ike would reply, "Freeman, I'll meet you on the 1st tee at Eldorado in half an hour." They had some wonderful times together.

The last time I saw him was at Walter Reed Hospital in Washington. I visited with him for about half an hour and then talked with Mamie for a while out in the hallway. As I was about to go, Mamie said, "You'd better say good-bye to Ike before you leave." As I walked back into his room I was trying to think of a joke to tell him, because I always told him every golf joke.

Ike looked tired, but he smiled when he saw me again. "Did you hear about the guy," I said, "despondent over his round, who walked into the locker room and loudly declared, 'I've got to be the worst golfer in the world.' There was another guy sitting there and he said, 'No, I am.'

"The first guy said, 'What did you have on the first hole?'

" 'An X.'

" 'You're one-up.' "

Ike laughed so hard I thought he was going to fall out of bed.

Six

Is There Any Hope?

After all the analysis and kidding I've done here about the golf skills of others, it's time to discuss my own game. At least what remains of it. Dolores says there are days when I'm closer to shooting my weight than my age, but the fact is I still work very hard on my game and I try to shoot the best score possible every time out. Even if I have to nudge the calculator a little now and then.

As I mentioned earlier, my handicap now is 20, the highest it's ever been. I think I'm actually about a 17 or 18 and with a little work I could get it back down to a 15. We all feel we're a little better than we actually are. A guy came into the locker room at Lakeside after playing one day and his friend asked him, "Did you shoot your usual game?" The man replied, "No, and come to think of it, I never have."

I'll shoot anywhere from 40 to 47 for 9 holes; for 18 it varies from the high 80s to the low and mid-90s. Sometimes my swing looks like a helicopter with a bad plug. I guess that's why MacGregor asked me if they could take their name off the balls I play.

The key to my game is the tee shot, and I suspect that's true for every senior player in the world. If I can get my drive into position, about two hundred yards out in the fairway, I can score. Otherwise each hole becomes an ordeal of defensive golf.

I'll hit the 4-iron about 150 yards, the 5-iron about 140, the 6-iron about 130 and so on. That's about 40 yards less than the average tour pro hits those irons, which gives you some ideas how long they are. I like to keep three or four fairway woods in my bag, hitting them anywhere from 150 to 190 yards. I never kick my ball in the rough or improve my lie in a sand trap. For that I have a caddie.

Like every senior golfer, I've lost a lot of distance over the years. In 1940, for example, my swing wasn't much different than it is today but I was much stronger. I could belt the ball pretty well in those days. My game probably reached its peak in the early 1950s, after Ben Hogan got me under his wing. My handicap at that time was 6 and I got it down to 4 for the British Amateur in 1951. And most of the time I knew where the ball was going.

Putting is the great variable in anyone's game. When I was younger I was a consistently good putter, leading with the left hand and stroking right through the ball. Crosby felt for years I was the best putter he'd seen. But Bing was often difficult to play with. After he won the Oscar for playing Father O'Malley in *Going My Way* he went out of control and wore his priest robe everywhere, even on the golf course. Have you ever tried to sink a ten-foot putt with your opponent clicking his rosary beads at you?

These days I tend to struggle on the greens. One day I'll hole everything I look at, the next day I'll start accelerating my backstroke and decelerating the stroke through the ball. All sorts of bad things can happen then. But I don't mind a few 3-putt greens if I'm hitting the ball crisply. There's nothing worse than laying two on the tee before you get past the ball washer.

Sam Snead once gave me a valuable putting tip. "Don't worry about the line, think more about the distance," Sam said. "Most of the 3-putting I see results from stroking the first putt either four feet short or four feet long. Try to get a good feel for the distance to the hole." Easy enough for Sam to say.

Based on all the lessons I've had if there is any one piece of advice I can pass along to golfers aged fifty and over it would be to maintain the extension of the backswing. As the years accumulate, the back muscles tend to constrict and it becomes increasingly hard to bring the club back into the proper position.

I'm fortunate in that on account of spending so much time on the stage, moving around and occasionally dancing a few steps, my back muscles haven't stiffened up that much. But I still have to concentrate on making a full turn. One day I was on the practice tee at Moor Park, in England, and Henry Cotton's wife, Toots, came over to me. She'd been watching Henry play and teach for years and really knew the golf swing. "You know, Bob," she told me, "you're not swinging long enough in the back." I knew what she meant.

Paul Runyan, a marvelous senior player and instructor, stresses the extension of the backswing in all his lessons. He even advocates a drill where the pupil tries to swing a rake. You can't really swing a rake, of course, but it does tend to slow down the backswing and strengthens your muscles in the process.

Another helpful tip came from Walter Hagen, one of the finest players of all time. "Drive that right knee at the target on the downswing," Walter would say. "You can't generate any real power without working the right knee." Watch Jack Nicklaus on the practice tee some time. I don't know if Jack ever knew Walter Hagen, but he exemplifies perfectly the technique of the working right knee.

Byron Nelson was the best I've seen at staying down on the ball during a shot. He kept his clubface on the ball longer than any pro of his time, maybe even longer than Lee Trevino does today. That's probably one reason Byron was so straight. I remember playing an exhibition with Byron at Kansas City in 1945, the year he won eleven straight tournaments. He took

---

Some might call this determination, but I admit it could be just panic. Whatever, my right arm appears to be somewhat limp on the follow-through. It could be the result of too many strokes on this particular day.

a divot with a 4-iron that was at least one foot long. I've never seen anything like it. Now that's staying down on the ball!

Claude Harmon, the 1948 Masters champion who taught for many years at Winged Foot, always stressed coordination. Coordinate your arms with the lower body. In other words, get your fanny out of the way on the downswing. It's also called throwing your hips, and that's how Claude described it. We were playing one day and I asked him, "How far do you throw your hip?" Claude said, "All the way across the street."

Nobody does that any better on the tour now than Johnny Miller. He really moves those hips, and stays down behind that ball. Watching Johnny hit iron shots is like watching a gifted artist at work. I played with Johnny and Jack Nicklaus in a charity match at the Kings Island complex in Cincinnati, where they hold the LPGA Championship. Nicklaus designed the course. Well, you've never seen two guys hit the ball like they did that day. It was just unbelievable. I was hitting the ball pretty well myself. On the 1st hole I was out 300 yards. Then I got out of the cart to hit my third shot.

Toney Penna, one of my dearest friends, gave me some good advice during the 1983 Desert Classic. Toney was riding around with me in the cart. "Noise," he kept saying, "make some noise." He meant making some noise with the driver as it comes into the ball. What he was actually saying was to get more clubhead speed, which is how you get more distance.

It was so typical of my game that I was bombing the wood shots that day and messing up the short irons and the chipping. You remember one hole where the TV cameras had caught us. Tip O'Neill hit his second shot into the water. Gerald Ford, next to hit, did the same thing. Well, of course I was thinking about that as I stood over the ball and naturally I landed mine into the water, too. It was pretty embarrassing. We all just stood there and laughed. What else could we do?

George Fazio taught me the cut shot. By that I mean hitting a little fade, left to right. Trevino does it beautifully. You get more control on your iron shots, those finesse shots into the green. George played that cut shot all the time.

I suppose the most complex instructor in the game today is Ben Doyle, who teaches at Carmel Valley on the Monterey Peninsula. Bobby Clampett works with him. Ben is a disciple of Homer Kelley's book *The Golfing Machine,* which is actually a physics book about golf. There are twenty-four key thoughts which the golfer must think about when he stands over

---

Lesson time for Crosby in proper sand shot technique. I don't know if Bing was impressed or falling asleep.

the ball. Can you believe that? I have trouble remembering one or two, let alone twenty-four. But Clampett swears by it and he's an awfully good young player.

I always take good care of the grips on my clubs, making sure they're clean and dry. You've got to have a grip than you can hold on to. I have my grips sandpapered a little, to rough them up. I've seen guys play where the club actually slipped out of their hands. Sometimes the club flew farther than the ball. That reminds of Sammy Davis. Sammy hits a nice ball, about 90 yards. But his jewelry flies 110. The trouble about playing golf with Sammy is that we always lose him in the ball washer.

Caddies are an important part of golf's tradition, and I've had some great ones over the years, but the truth is that now I'd rather ride around the course. I prefer to drive the cart myself. I'm trying to find a golf cart that's very light and won't leave any tracks on the green, so I won't have to get out of the cart to putt. I really enjoy riding in a golf cart, and just recently I had an exceptionally good day. I only fell out of the cart twice.

In this game you run into a lot of strange handicaps. There's the guy who carries a 4, for the sake of prestige, but he's really a 14. He's easy money. Then there's the 4 masquerading as a 14. His picture belongs on the post office wall. Just the other day I was playing a guy like that. I said I was a 20 and he said he was a 20. What a liar he was. I had to shoot 68 to beat him.

But I really admire a guy who can play to his low handicap. Jim Garner hovered between a 2 and a 5 at Riviera for years and seldom lost money. My friend, the late Pardee Erdman, was a 2 at Pebble Beach and that's pretty strong. I played with Father Durkin one year at the Crosby. I forget what his handicap was, but it was fairly low and he played to it. He wasn't all that impressed by my game, however. I had him bless my clubs and I dropped $20 in the poor box. When he saw my swing he gave me back the $20 and dropped my clubs in the poor box.

One course where only low handicappers should play is Sawgrass, near Jacksonville, Florida. They held the Tournament Players Championship there several times and the scores were astronomical. I gave it a run in the pro-am of the TPC, and quickly discovered that Sawgrass separates the men from the boys. It was a great feeling being a boy again. On one hole I hit an alligator so hard that he's now my golf bag.

Perfect form, ideal concentration at the Los Angeles Open a few years ago. Now this is what I call extension on the backswing! As I recall, I double-bogeyed this hole.

Dr. Cary Middlecoff once analyzed my swing for *Golf Digest*. Among his observations were that I had a ham-handed grip and should develop more flex in my knees. Crosby read that and remarked that I can't start my swing until my knees start knocking. He added that about the best thing he could say about my swing was that it had a one-piece wobble.

I've been playing in front of galleries so long it never affects my game. I'm such a ham I usually hit my best drives on the 1st and 10th tees, where the galleries are the largest. But I do remember coming up to the 9th green in the pro-am of the Dinah Shore tournament and hitting the worst shank you've ever seen. I thought about Crosby, looking down watching me, after blowing that shot. Bing always said my swing looked like Grandma Moses trying to keep warm.

No matter. The only thing that counts in golf is the final number on the scorecard. I always keep my own score. I mark it correctly, to the best of my knowledge. But with all the strokes I take on a hole, I think I can be forgiven if I forget one . . . or two . . . but one time I went too far. I made a hole in one and marked down a zero.

Speaking of holes in one, I've made five. The one I remember best was on the 8th hole at Bob O'Link, a men's club in Chicago where I belonged for about twelve years. Dick Gibson and Hugh Davis were with me that day. Scotty Fessenden had signed us up as members one night a few years earlier when we were drinking at the bar after I had shot 74.

My last ace was shot on the 5th hole at Butler National in Chicago on August 20, 1974, shortly after Butler had opened. The 5th is a killer, 220 yards long, practically surrounded by water. I was playing with George Fazio, who had designed the course; Frank Sullivan, one of my attorneys; and Red Harbour, who, along with Paul Butler, had founded the club. Butler was riding along in a golf cart with us.

The other three guys had all knocked their tee shots on the green when I stepped up and took out a driver. I just barely cleared the water, the ball landing in the front right corner of the green and rolling up and into the cup, which was cut back in the left rear corner. It was the first hole in one at the new course, and to commemorate it they put up a plaque at the 5th green, which is still there. It was a fun day.

Chicago's a great golf town. The Western Open is played each year at Butler National, benefiting the Evans Caddie Scholarship program that was

---

Ben Hogan always taught me to maintain a high follow-through. He never warned me that if my club got any higher I'd be climbing a tree.

instituted by Chick Evans, the great amateur who spent his entire life living in Chicago. It may have more great courses than any one city in the country. One day I was playing with Irv Kupcinet, the Chicago columnist and he 4-putted a green. As we walked to the next hole I said, "You 4-putted the last green." Irv said, "I know—I like to putt."

Irv shouldn't have felt badly about that. I saw Tommy Armour 4-putt a green during the 1935 U.S. Open at Oakmont. Tommy was so mad I thought he was going to destroy himself.

Some of my golf partners are getting up in years now. Like the ninety-five-year-old fellow I played with last year. He beat me, and as I was paying him off I asked him, "Are you really ninety-five?" He said, "Yes, but I'm falling apart. Like yesterday, I said to my girlfriend, 'Let's make a little love.' She said, 'But we just did, ten minutes ago.' You see what I mean? I'm losing my memory."

Andy Williams and I play about the same caliber of golf. He's a fun guy to have in the group. Andy carries his own bag and the caddie carries his change of sweaters. Dean Martin's a little better than Andy or myself. I've seen Deano send a ball over 250 yards . . . just by breathing on it.

I had a good time, and played reasonably well as I recall, in Roy Clark's celebrity tournament. It's the only golf event I know where your caddie is a mule. You should have seen all the country music stars at the pro-am gala. I was the only man backstage wearing low heels. Roy is the perfect host. You not only get a starting time, you get a downbeat. Roy played extremely well that day. He was hitting the ball so hard he knocked three rhinestones off his 4-wood.

Jimmy Stewart could have been a good golfer, but he speaks so slowly that by the time he yells "Fore!" the guy he's hit is already in an ambulance on the way to the hospital.

As amateurs we all get nervous in tight situations on the course, but I've noticed that the pros do, too. Craig Stadler was obviously very jumpy playing the final hole when he won the Desert Classic in 1980. I was standing next to Tom Seaver as Stadler came onto the green and I said, "Man, is he uptight. He's about to burst." Seaver, who has known the pressure of pitching in the World Series, smiled and replied, "You'd be uptight, too, if you were playing for $50,000."

I once made a terrible mistake driving my golf car out ahead of my foursome while Jerry Ford was hitting behind me. That isn't curiosity written all over my face— just sheer terror.

The next year I was standing by Rex Caldwell, who was leading Keith Fergus by one stroke, when Fergus looked over his birdie putt on the last hole. Rex was so fidgety he couldn't say a word. He just stood there, frozen, watching Fergus line up his putt. Keith made the long one to force the play-off and then beat Rex on the first extra hole. Caldwell later said that he would never submit himself to that ordeal again . . . that if it ever came up, he would walk away so he wouldn't have to watch the putt.

Look what happened to Bobby Clampett and Nick Price in the 1982 British Open, at Troon. Clampett was walking away with the tournament after 36 holes. Then he collapsed. Price had a 3-stroke lead with 6 holes to play and lost it to Tom Watson. Pressure. The pros feel it just like we do. I was delighted to see Nick Price come back and win the World Series of Golf in 1983, on that great Firestone course.

I watch all the golf on television. I don't mean just the Masters and the U.S. Open, but all the pro tour events, week after week. I love it. I was there in front of the tube when Arnold Palmer beat Ken Venturi for the Masters in 1960 with that great finish, then Palmer won the Open a couple of months later while driving the first hole on the last round, Venturi's heroic triumph in the Open at Congressional in 1964, Palmer blowing the Open to Casper in 1966 at Olympic, the scorecard thing at the 1968 Masters involving Goalby and de Vicenzo, Nicklaus at Pebble Beach in 1972 . . . you name it. I saw Weiskopf win the Western Open with the closing birdie in '82, Gary Koch holding on to win the rain-drenched Doral Open in '83, the long play-off between Jim Colbert and Fuzzy Zoeller at the Colonial in '83.

One of the most exciting performances I've ever seen on a TV screen had to be Johnny Miller's 63 in the final round of the Open at Oakmont in 1973. That was absolutely unbelievable. Oakmont may be the second most difficult golf course in the country, just behind Pebble Beach, and for Johnny to shoot that kind of score under Open conditions just defies description. I know what a real accomplishment that was because I've played Oakmont. A photographer kept shooting me every time I swung. I was very flattered until I found out he was from *Field and Stream*.

A play-off I'll never forget was the one between Jack Nicklaus and Lee Elder at the American Golf Classic in Akron in 1968. Not many remember it started out as a three-way contest, but Frank Beard fell out on the 1st

---

Succumbing to an irresistible impulse during an exhibition I played at Ansley Park in Atlanta years ago with Dot Kirby, Louise Suggs and Lieutenant Colonel T. S. Rawlings. Those butterflies in the next fairway kept distracting me on the greens.

hole and then Lee and Jack started trading long putts. Lee looked like he had the thing locked up several times, but Jack kept coming up with the clutch putts and he finally took it away from Lee after 5 holes of sudden death.

When the U.S. Open is on they give you four hours each on Saturday and Sunday and I never leave the chair. I was mesmerized watching Nicklaus and Aoki going head to head those last two rounds at Baltusrol in 1980, each coming up with incredible shots.

It's those fabulous shots under pressure that I remember the most. Like Jerry Pate hitting that 5-iron across the water, a shot that was heard all around the bank, to win the Open at Atlanta in 1976, or Hale Irwin gunning that 2-iron to the green on the last hole of the Open at Winged Foot in '74. I almost fell over watching Bob Gilder make that double eagle at Westchester in 1982. He holed a wood shot from 251 yards, a shot the TV cameras caught perfectly. The ball dived right into the hole. What got me was Gilder was 251 yards from the pin and used a 3-wood. From that distance I use a cannon. And then a year later, on the same hole, Seve Ballesteros got an eagle 3 on the final round to with the tournament. Those are the shots that identify the great champions of golf.

The battle between Fuzzy Zoeller and Greg Norman in the 1984 U.S. Open at Winged Foot was delightful to watch. Who could ever forget Norman making that incredible par on the 72nd hold and Fuzzy, standing back in the fairway, waving that white towel in mock surrender. That was a memorable moment for golf. It showed that the game's leading players, in the grinding pressure of the crunch, can have a sense of humor, too.

Norman is a fabulous ball-striker. He was practicing one day at Bay Hill near Orlando, Florida, where he and his wife Laura have built a new home. He was hitting some tee shots in the general direction of the Atlantic Ocean and after one boomer, Cuba fired back.

Golf is such an enjoyable sport to watch on television. They give you the replays of all the key shots, the instructional tips and the interviews with the winners. President Reagan even calls the winners from time to time, offering his congratulations. I knew the President would run for reelection in 1984. Why not? Actors love sequels . . . and reruns.

Lee Trevino's natural warmth and perceptive observations on NBC have added a great deal to golf on television. It's not easy being up in that tower behind the 18th green with the anchorman. You don't want to butt in, step

---

My old sidekick Jerry Colonna and a set of clubs so ancient they've become classics.

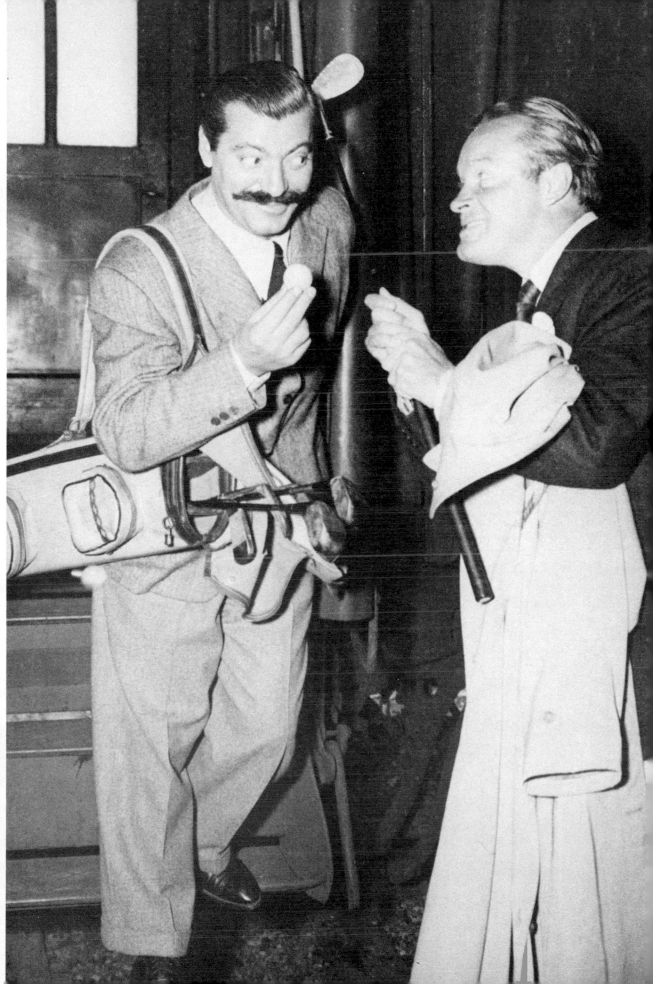

Ike and a couple of top singers at the Desert Classic, 1966. Andy Williams had crossed the "Moon River" by that time and me—well, I'm just thankful for the memories.

A trifle quick on the release in the bunker at Memphis in 1973. I've listened to many different pros discussing technique in the sand, but for me I have only one covenant—get it out. I made it out of there, but just barely.

Who says golf is a sedentary game? Here I'm playing at a dead run in San Francisco with a group of sports writers. Under those conditions you can distract the gallery enough so they don't remember your score.

on his lines, but still you're expected to contribute and I think Lee does an outstanding job.

Whenever I watch golf on television I want to race over to Lakeside and either hit balls or play 9 holes. In recent years I've gotten more involved in the mechanics of the game. This is probably a natural reaction for senior players because as you get older your skills erode and you need that extra edge to keep sharp.

Practice is the key. Wherever I went to entertain our troops overseas I always brought along my clubs. Those long plane rides stiffened my muscles to the point where I could never go out and play the next day without warming up first. So now, whenever I play, I always hit a bucket of balls first. You never see a pro play without first warming up, so how could we amateurs expect to play well without doing the same thing?

But isn't golf a fabulous game, whether you're playing or watching on television? On the course you've got a built-in insulation against committing a blunder in public. If you drop the pass in football, or miss the shot in basketball, or strike out in baseball, everybody knows it. If you hit a bad shot in golf, you can always claim you know a shortcut to the green. At least that's my story.

It's very difficult to stick my nose out and list the best courses I've played. I've enjoyed them all, even on the day in Vail, Colorado, in 1982 when I was playing with Fuzzy Zoeller in Gerald Ford's tournament in the fall and it was so cold I was taking ice divots. Fuzzy asked me if I wanted to quit. I told him, "No, I'm no quitter." He said, "I guess you'd rather be a Birds Eye golfer." It was obvious he wanted to mother me, so I quit.

Lakeside is a very special course for me and so is Cypress Point. I joined Cypress a long time ago and haven't played nearly as many rounds there as I would have wished. It's such a beautiful place. A very low-keyed club, with some of the country's leading businessmen as members. It's also very exclusive. Cypress had a very successful membership drive last month. They drove out forty members.

But what a gorgeous golf course. It measures only 6,505 yards from the back tees, very short for a championship track in modern times. Every hole is an unforgettable experience. The most recent one for me occurred on the 7th hole, a par 3 of 163 yards. The green, however, tilts sharply from the back to the front. In my last round there I hit a tee shot about thirteen feet above the hole and 3-putted. A smart pro would have left his tee shot below the hole.

Cypress Point opened on August 11, 1928. It was designed by Alister Mackenzie, who also built the Augusta National course, and financed by a group of investors that included Roger Lapham and Marion Hollins, one of the outstanding women players of that time. They got the 170 acres from the Del Monte Properties Company for $150,000, which wouldn't even buy the first hole today. They were planning to add tennis courts and a swimming pool, but the stock market crash in October of 1929 took care of that. You won't find a more pervasive golf atmosphere anywhere. I just wish I'd have more time to play there.

But once you get hooked on golf, that's it. A friend of mine, a great golfer, was shipwrecked on this island for three months. Finally he looked out and saw what he thought was a mirage—a beautiful girl in a canoe. But it was a beautiful girl in a canoe. She walked up on the beach and asked him, "How long have you been here?" The guy said, "Three months."

The girl said, "Would you like a cigarette?"

"Would I," the man replied. She took a cigarette out of her bra and handed it to him. Then she asked him if he'd like a little scotch. The guy said, "Would I," so she took a little bottle of scotch out of her bra and handed it to him.

As he lit that cigarette and sipped that scotch, the girl sidled up to him and asked, "Would you like to play around?"

"Don't tell me you have golf clubs in there."

Seven

Don't Cancel That Reservation

Just the other day someone asked me how often I play golf. I was curious myself, so I went through my files of the previous year and it turned out that I had either played or hit balls nearly three hundred times. With all that practice I really should play better, but I actually hit my most creative shots with a pencil. I need scorecards that are not allergic to erasers.

Most of my golf is over the 9-hole route, because I simply don't have enough time for more. Occasionally I'll go 18, mostly at pro-ams on the PGA Tour or in Gerald Ford's tournament each year at Vail.

My lifestyle hasn't changed much over the years. When I'm at home in North Hollywood I work nearly every day. But unless I'm taping a television commercial, which consumes an entire afternoon, I'll drive over to Lakeside, five minutes away, and either hit balls or play 9 holes. On Sunday afternoons I generally play 9 with Dolores.

If it's chilly or raining, I'll take a two-hour nap about five o'clock. There's nothing like a late-afternoon snooze to make a guy feel really good, especially at my age. But I still dream about birdies.

At seven o'clock my masseur comes in for a forty-five minute rubdown and at eight I have dinner. Afterwards it's back to work. I can get a lot more done in the evening, when the phones aren't ringing. I'll dictate letters, return some calls and occasionally hop over to NBC, less than ten minutes away, to work on the next show. I try to get to bed by one o'clock in the morning, and get up the next morning at ten.

I follow pretty much the same routine when we're in Palm Springs, which averages out to about forty days a year. I play my golf there at several desert clubs, usually Canyon or Eldorado. They're within fifteen minutes of the house we built five years ago, on a hillside property overlooking Palm Springs. It's got twenty-five thousand square feet of space and all sorts of handy gadgets. It took me a long time to learn how to operate them. For the first three years whenever I flushed the toilet the garage door would fly open.

At Lakeside my most frequent golfing companions are old pals like Bob O'Brien, Glen Campbell, Bobby Hamilton or Dick Gibson. Gibson is a broker. He sometimes gets the stock prices mixed up with my score. He also has the longest golf clubs I've ever seen, even longer than Crosby's. Dick could stay home and still play. I can't overlook Bones Maloncy, who's another Lakeside crony.

At Palm Springs it's usually Bob Bremson, Paul Jenkins, Gerald Ford or Jack Koennecker, who recently retired as the pro at Canyon. Koennecker has been helping me a great deal with my game. He gave me a new sequence for playing the short irons. It's a basic one-two-three timing: one for the backswing, two for the downswing and three for the follow-through. Koennecker believes the follow-through is a critically important element of the swing. We were watching the Masters on TV one day and on the 15th hole, the par 5 with water just in front of the green, Jack Nicklaus dumped his little wedge shot into the pond. "See there," Koennecker shouted. "He didn't follow through on that swing and look what happened."

We usually play the 9 holes for $5.00, just enough to keep your interest sharp. Ford and I sometimes play for $5.00 a hole. The President has to give me two strokes and I can tell you that there are easier ways to make a living than playing against him.

Jack Hennessy and I have been playing together quite a bit at Palm Springs since he built a home at the Vintage Club, a beautiful new course that Tom Fazio designed. Shortly after they moved into their new home, Jack and his wife Shirlee had the damndest experience. It was a Friday, and the maid had just left for the weekend. They walked into one of the rooms and the door locked behind them. There was no way to get out. Jack's golf bag happened to be in that room. He took out his wedge and smashed a hole through the wall. Otherwise they'd have been stuck there until the maid returned on Monday. I told Jack it was the best wedge shot he ever hit.

While it's true that I play for modest stakes on the golf course now, there was a day when big money was riding on the line. Years ago Crosby and I were going to play in the pro-am of the Phoenix Open. He suggested we travel to Phoenix by train, since Bing didn't care to fly at that time. He introduced me to a friend who would play with us the next day. It was Del Webb, the industrialist who would later build Sun City in Arizona, a couple of big hotels in Las Vegas and Lake Tahoe and become part owner of the New York Yankees. I had never met him. "Don't worry," Bing assured me. "He's a pigeon. You'll beat him like a drum."

We played a $100 nassau, meaning $100 for each 9, with automatic presses. Del shot 73 on the Phoenix Country Club course and I took a bath.

That was the beginning, however, of a long friendship with Del Webb. We played a lot of golf all over the country, mostly for big stakes. Our standard game was for $25 a hole with all sorts of little side bets and we usually went double or nothing on the 18th tee. I got even with him but good one day at Lakeside. After 17 holes he owed me $875 and on the 18th, of course, it was double or nothing.

The 18th hole at Lakeside is a strong par 4, measuring about four hundred yards. We both hit good drives. On my second shot I hooked a 4-wood just left of the green, and a little short. Del was on the front edge of the green with a 3-iron. I was going to hit a wedge for my third, but I switched to a 9-iron and rolled it into the cup for a birdie 3. Del, who hardly ever swore, glowered at me and said, "Hope, you sunnuva bitch!" I got him for over $1,700. (If the IRS is reading, they should figure this as fiction.)

Del was an ardent gin player. We were having lunch one day in Los Angeles and I told him I was flying commercial later in the afternoon to Phoenix. "I'll fly you over," Del said. He had a Beechcraft Bonanza. He

Fore on the right, in a warm-up for the pro-am of the Byron Nelson Classic in 1979. The President and I forgot to synchronize our swings.

wanted me to play gin, still thinking about that $1,700-plus he had lost to me at Lakeside. I think we about broke even with the cards on that flight.

Jackie Gleason likes to gamble on the golf course. The first time we played, for $100 a hole, he took me pretty good. But I got so I could beat him nearly every time. One day we were playing in the pro-am of the Memorial Tournament at Muirfield Village near Columbus, Ohio, Jack Nicklaus' tournament. On the 14th hole, a short par 4 with water on the right, Gleason was on the green in three. I was knocking around in the traps and finally got on in 4. I made the putt for a 5, Jackie 3-putted for a 6. The carry-over bet on that hole was $1,000. I tapped him for about $1,400 that day, which almost got me even with him for the year. After a while we started to pay off after each hole, because we tended to get our score and our finances confused. We'd whip out the money on the next tee, much to the delight of the gallery.

Speaking of golf gambits, I learned a new one recently. It's called Free Throw. A guy I was playing with said to me, "I'll give you a stroke on this hole if you'll give me a free throw." It sounded like a pretty good deal to me until we arrived on the green and he picked up my ball and threw it into a lake. I never forgave Crosby for that.

There's nothing like a round of golf to take your mind off shows, business deals or taping television commercials. I love to play anywhere. Hot weather doesn't bother me, as long as I'm riding a cart. In September of 1983 I played the Fox Theater in St. Louis for a week and I was out on the golf course nearly every day, even when the temperatures were pushing a hundred degrees. I've also played at Vancouver in windbreakers, the Crosby in ski jackets and in Korea in a coat so heavy I could hardly swing.

The most enjoyable golf is always in Palm Springs, because the courses there are so beautifully conditioned and the rough is negligible. I don't play well out of the rough. Scottish golf is great, but St. Andrews and Gleneagles have traps where you get in and you're never heard from again.

Two delightful newer Palm Springs courses are the Vintage Club and Morningside. Morningside, located adjacent to the Springs Club, is a Nicklaus course. It's absolutely gorgeous. Nicklaus, incidentally, is becoming such a prolific golf architect that he's got new projects going everywhere. I finally found a spot where he hadn't built one—in a leper colony.

Getting a little help on a tough putt from Del Webb, in 1949. Del was part owner of the Yankees and felt that anyone from Cleveland needed all the assistance he could get.

Nicklaus was only ten years old when an incident occurred that made me realize how much I truly love golf. It was 1950, and I was making the movie *Fancy Pants* with Lucille Ball. Dick Gibson and I had planned to play after the day's shooting had been completed at Paramount. I had one scene left, in which I was riding a horse.

These were close-up shots, so instead of a real horse they used a prop horse, a mechanical gadget. The director wanted more action, so they loosened the straps on the horse and speeded up the action. I was flipped backwards off the horse, head over teakettle. They carried me off the lot in a stretcher, and as they put me into a car, I said, "Right to Lakeside, please." I wound up in Presbyterian Hospital for eight weeks. It was a long time to be away from golf.

The next time I played was at Bob O'Link, a men's club in Chicago. The others in the group were Dick Gibson, Hugh Davis and Dick Sniderman. We had started on the back 9, so by the time we reached the 8th hole, which was our 17th, the bets were rolling. I hit a little faded 5-iron on the hole, which measured 150 yards, and knocked it into the cup for an ace. There is still a plaque on that tee commemorating that feat. I also shot 74 that day, which wasn't bad for a refugee from the hospital.

Gibson and I have had adjacent lockers at Lakeside for nearly fifty years. Dick's always been a great pal, and a frequent business associate. He got me into some good oil deals with Crosby, and Monty Moncrief. Dick's a good man.

Speaking of finances, *Forbes* magazine reported in an article about the four hundred wealthiest people in the United States that I was worth $200 million. Now that's really ridiculous. They put the decimal point in the wrong place.

It made about as much sense as the bit in *Time* magazine's cover story on me in 1967 when they asked a fellow backstage what he thought I was worth and he said about half a billion dollars. Les Brown showed me the magazine in Bangkok, when we were doing a tour show. I wired the editor and said, "If you can find it, I'll split it with you."

If I had that kind of money I'd have bought my own jet long ago. I did think about it. Now when I get on a commercial flight some guy, who has obviously read *Forbes* and *Time,* will look at me and ask, "Is this your plane?" I'll say, "Yes—one seat."

I can't imagine my life without traveling. I've been going strong in the air for over fifty years, flying on everything from Concordes to a one-passenger prop. These days I average about a hundred days a year on the road.

I like to sit in the right window seat in the first row. The flight attendants see to it that nobody bothers me, and pretty soon I've dozed off. The next

I've never set a course record, but I have the honor of scoring a hole in one at the Bob O'Link Club in Chicago. I remember it happened on the 8th hole and I was playing with two great pals, Dick Gibson and Hugh Davis. I got my last one in Chicago, too, at Butler National.

One of the great players of all time and his bag of burglar tools. Those sticks have been all over the world, and have 3-putted in so many countries I couldn't keep count.

thing I know we're landing in New York. My friend Bill Fugazy has a limo there to pick me up and off we go to the Waldorf Towers. Fugazy is a big transportation man. I think he arranged the last tour for Amelia Earhart.

Whenever possible I prefer to take a corporate jet. It's like riding in the club car. The jet is usually provided by the company I'm doing an appearance for, or by an associate of them. Alex Spanos, who has extensive land and building holdings throughout the country, has a couple of jets I often use. I don't pick on him much, but I do beg occasionally. Alex, a fine golfer, recently bought the San Diego Chargers of the National Football League. Poor man. He had to open two piggy banks to do it.

Compared with taking commercial flights from the Los Angeles airport, it's so much simpler to travel by corporate jet. I drive from my home in North Hollywood to the Burbank airport, about twelve minutes away, climb in and away we go. No metal detector, and I'm glad. The stays in my corset would delay me too long.

My routine on the road doesn't differ much from mine at home. Up at 10 A.M. and on the phone. A light lunch, and off to the golf course. The great thing about traveling is that I can see so many friends each year. Like Bill Fugazy in New York, Francis Sullivan in Philadelphia, Pat Casey in Milwaukee, Father Paul Reinert in St. Louis. I often play with Jack (Loveball) Hausman at Deepdale on Long Island, where I've been a member for thirty-five years. Fugazy is one of the stalwarts at Winged Foot. He has a big limo business. I always kid him about the time in 1976 when I was appearing at his All-American College Golf Foundation dinner at the Waldorf. Nancy Lopez, who was then still a college golfer and one of the best-known women amateur golfers in the country, was also on the program. Nancy had to fly in from an amateur tournament in North Carolina. One of Fugazy's limos was to meet her at the Newark airport. Nancy had to go extra holes in a match, however, and missed the flight. She caught one about two hours later. When she got to Newark, no limo. She was all set to board a return flight to Winston-Salem when the problem was resolved and a limo showed up. Nancy appeared on the podium in her golf skirt and sweater and Fugazy was able at last to relax.

After the golf round I go back to the suite, shower and have a nice dinner in the room. Then I rest for a while, go over to the theater and come on stage about 9 P.M. for an hour or so of fun, playing to a great audience. My limo is waiting at the back door and when I get back to the hotel I always take a long, brisk walk with a driver in my hand. Someone asked me if I would take my driver to heaven with me. I said no, I better not because I had that club in my hands when I said too many nasty things about Him.

Just before going to bed I usually have a bowl of ice cream, provided by my friend Tom Carvel. Carvel makes the best ice cream in the world. The price is right, too.

One year I delivered the commencement address at Oral Roberts University in Tulsa, the West Point for civilians. Before we played golf that afternoon Oral touched my putter. But it didn't do any good. I'm still short. He must have touched the wrong side.

It's tough to find much time for golf when I do my college tour, because I'm in and out in a day. But at the University of Florida I did a show in the football stadium, in front of sixty thousand people, and made my entrance in a golf cart. They didn't know I came right from the course.

I try to squeeze in short vacations here and there, like stopping off in Hawaii for a few days on the way home from a tour in Australia last year. That was terrific. Recently Dolores and I spent a wonderful R and R at the Lodge at Pebble Beach with Dr. Bob Ellsworth and his wife Gracie. Dr. Ellsworth is my eye man at The New York Hospital and a member at the Knickerbocker Club in New Jersey. I shot a 92 at Cypress Point and a 93 at Pebble Beach.

It was the fulfillment of a longtime wish. I've always loved Pebble Beach, although it's just too much golf course for me. I've been a member at Cypress Point for about thirty-five years and except for my appearances there in the Crosby tournament I doubt if I had played the course five times. It's a beautiful spot, best eulogized by Frank ("Sandy") Tatum of San Francisco, former president of the United States Golf Association, as the Sistine Chapel of golf.

Usually we play these rounds in privacy, but there was the time not long ago when I traveled to Meadville, Pennsylvania, to perform at the county fair. Ray Shafer, the former governor of Pennsylvania and now the head of the USO, had arranged a golf game in Meadville. The local populace had apparently been tipped off, because when we got to the golf course there were four hundred people surrounding the 1st tee. Ray apologized to me about the crowd, but I didn't mind. A crowd always brings out the ham in me, and some of it even gets to my clubs.

People often ask me about my golf equipment. Well, for about thirty years I was a MacGregor man. I got them from Toney Penna, who was MacGregor's top club designer and later founded his own company. Then Ben Hogan gave me a set. And Jack Nicklaus. Now I've got about twenty sets and I try them all, still looking for that miracle set.

My golf clubs got a good bouncing around recently on a trip to Alaska. It was a rocky flight, at night, and we had to come in with the help of searchlights. The landing strip was so icy that we finally touched down on a grassy area. My first words after stepping off the plane were "I want to thank the greenkeeper who mowed the runways."

Seattle World's Fair, 1962. I went backstage between shows to work on my swing and this little guy came along to watch, and instruct on my grip. The picture was so great I used it on the cover of my program for personal appearances.

It was so cold that I thought we'd discovered God's frozen people. But there was a golf course nearby, and off we went. An old guy came up and said he'd like to caddie for me and the man I was playing with. I said OK. He picked up the two bags and hustled off to the 1st tee. I asked him how old he was and he said ninety-four. I said that was amazing. He replied, "Oh, this is nothing. I'm getting married tomorrow." I said, "Why would you want to get married at ninety-four?" He looked at me defiantly and said, "Who wants to?"

On my trips to the Washington, D.C., area I always look up my son Tony. Tony was a fine golfer as a youngster. He took lessons from Ed Dudley at the Broadmoor in Colorado Springs. Tony could drive the ball 250 yards or more. Then he sort of lost interest in golf, because his girlfriend loved tennis. And Tony loved her, so now they have two of my grandchildren. Tony is playing golf again since his teenage son Zachary has taken up the game. Zachary is going to be a really fine golfer. You feel the years catching up when you have to play like hell to beat your grandson.

Which reminds me of the guy sitting in the dining room at his golf club looking out the window at the practice green, where his son was putting. The man said to his lunch companion at the table, "Look at my son out there. He made me a millionaire." The other man said, "Really?" and the fellow replied, "Yes. I used to be a multi."

For many of the show business people who live in the Los Angeles area, Las Vegas is a popular place to work. It's close by, the money is good and there is plenty of diversion at the casino tables. I've played a lot of golf in Las Vegas, but I've always resisted the offers to work a show there. I wouldn't take those silicone shots for anything. Besides, I'm a lousy gambler. When I'm $4.00 down I look like I'm in the middle of open heart surgery.

Lord knows I still travel enough, but maybe one reason I'm a little more selective is that I'm so darn busy in Los Angeles. I do several television shows a year for NBC, and they take a great deal of time. Rehearsals, taping, editing . . . it requires an enormous amount of work to produce an hour's show. Counting radio, I've been with NBC for about forty-five years. When I started out with the network, General David Sarnoff was using the enlisted men's washroom.

I've enjoyed doing those television commercials, for example with Texaco. They take time, however, and on those days there's no golf for me. When I'm taping commercials, it's impossible for me to do anything else. It's not like a personal appearance. Then I can play golf, because I know my act and I can ad-lib some stuff. But in taping I have to pay attention. There are so many details.

A one-minute commercial can take up to three hours to complete. I do it over and over again, because Texaco has regional ads on TV and they

Jane Russell and I were filming Paleface *when this one was taken. I don't know what tepee I'm looking at, but General Omar Bradley seems to be enjoying the scene.*

My fan club in Washington, D.C., circa 1949.

change words for different parts of the country. Whenever I see a commercial on my calendar that day I just blot out the entire afternoon. But on nontaping days I force time for golf. About five o'clock I'll get in my car and one of my secretaries will chase me down the driveway, saying, "What about so-and-so? When can you fit him in?" By that time I'm headed around the corner for Lakeside.

I have mentioned the problem of signing autographs in public places, like airports, theaters, restaurants or on the golf course. Lakeside is one place I never have to think about that. I'm one of the guys there. Away from the club I must sign 350 autographs a day, which is not really difficult. The hard part is trying to give them to people.

The strangest place I've ever been asked for an autograph is at the urinal in the men's room. I looked over and told the guy, "Pal, if you'll just let me finish, I'll sign it for you." But I'm always nice to my fans. Without them I'd have to do it the hard way . . . with talent.

Sports has always been a big part of my life. I watch all the pro football and baseball I can on television, and just about every golf telecast. I used to attend many of the games, but not so much anymore. It's just too much of a hassle.

Years ago Dolores and I chartered two buses to the Rose Bowl game every New Year's Day. After the game we had about two hundred of our friends over to the house for food and drinks. One time I noticed there were several people I didn't know. I walked over to a guy wearing a sweatshirt nibbling on the shrimp and asked him who he was and how he happened to be there. "I'm a friend of the bus driver," he said. "He asked me." That was our last Rose Bowl party.

I used to be a part owner of the Los Angeles Rams and I still kick myself thinking about the chance I turned down to buy the entire thing for $12 million. When Dan Reeves and Ed Pauley were majority owners I had 11 percent. Dan and Ed weren't getting along very well, they wouldn't even sit together at the games in fact, and eventually Dan bought out Ed's share for $7 million. Dan asked me to be his partner, but I was a friend of Ed and Dan both and I just didn't think it was right to side with one of them. Then Dan died and I had the opportunity to become sole owner. But I was so busy doing this and that and I never got around to it. Dumb, dumb. Now the franchise is worth about $60 million.

That was about twenty years ago. What I should have done was to buy the Rams and sell my share of the Cleveland Indians baseball team. The Indians haven't had a winning team for a long time. But I still follow the Indians and maybe someday they'll be back up there, like they were in 1948 and 1954.

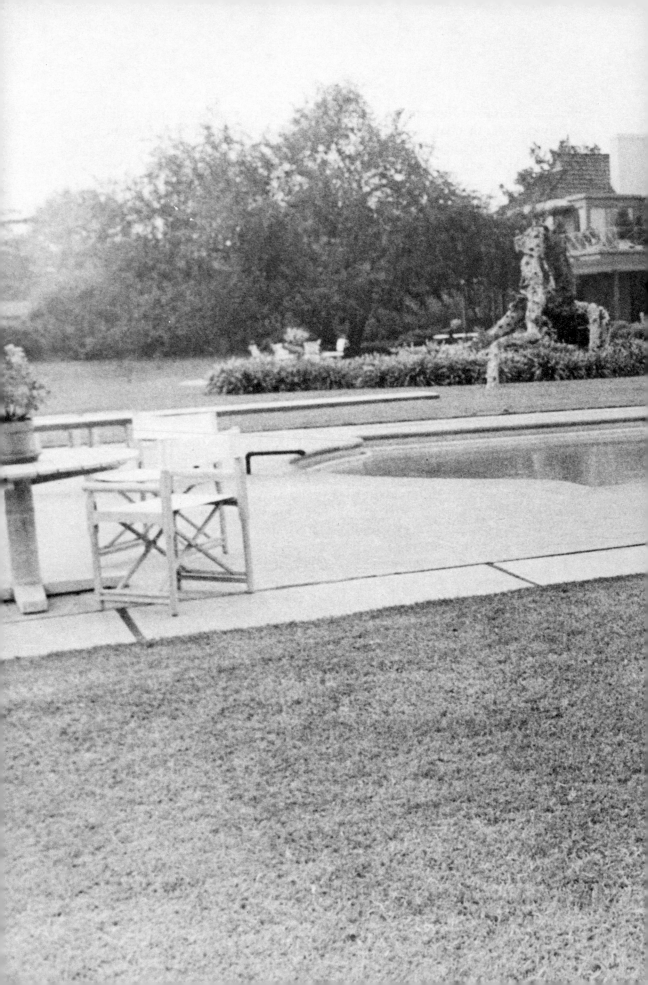

Being a club owner gives you a feeling that you're competing, which is one thing I really don't do much more in golf. I mean on a tournament level. I remember a particular round with Ben Hogan and General Omar Bradley at the Army-Navy Golf Club in Washington. The general was keeping score for our group and when the round was over he said, "Bob, I've got you for a 73. That's terrific." 73? I said, "General, did you count them all?" He said, "That's what I have you for."

General Bradley was a fine player, very strong. He was about a 9-handicapper and very competitive on the course.

For several years I played in the Lakeside club championship but don't remember ever getting past the first round. But now I prefer just to play social golf with friends unless I'm in a pro-am or something. I love golfing in L.A. because there's always someone interesting to play with. Not long ago I had a game with Burt Reynolds. Burt wanted to make it a foursome so he called Dolly Parton.

I miss so many of the guys who aren't around anymore . . . Bing, Ike, General Bradley, Pardee Erdman, Bill Stern, Ted Husing and writers like Grantland Rice, Bill Corum, Red Smith, Linc Werden, Braven Dyer. Rice spent a lot of time around Lakeside. Everybody liked him.

Tennis has become a popular sport for many of my pals in show business. I played tennis as a kid, but I probably haven't been on a court in sixty-five years. I'm not sure if it's all that beneficial for a man my age. The beauty of golf is that you can play it long after you have to give up other sports.

I like the story of the old-timer who could still hit the ball pretty well but couldn't see where it went. He had a hard time getting a game. One day the pro told him, "Charlie I've got just the right partner for you. Tom's about your age and he's got eyes like a hawk."

So the two guys got together and on the 1st tee Charlie hit his drive, turned to Tom and asked, "Did you see it?"

Tom: "Yes."

Charlie: "Where did it go?"

Tom: "I forgot."

Relaxing on the lawn at my home on Toluca Lake in North Hollywood. That pool is about the only water hazard I've missed in over 50 years of golf. But just to make sure, my practice balls are all floatable.

Some consider it remarkable that at this stage of life I'm able to maintain such a busy pace. They ask me when I'm going to retire. Retire? This is work? Play golf, tell a few jokes and have so many friends all over the world? My whole career has been a round of golf.

I gave some thought to retiring about twenty years ago when I developed problems in my left eye. I was sitting with Jane Russell backstage in Long Beach one night and suddenly I felt dizzy. The eye was hemorrhaging. I had four operations, and missed a lot of golf, before that was cleared up.

In 1979 I was appearing on a television show in Columbus to commemorate the fiftieth anniversary of the Ohio Theater. Gerald and Betty Ford were there, along with Ginger Rogers, Vic Damone, Lillian Gish, Woody Hayes and Governor Jim Rhodes. I was doing my routine of the song "Lazy," which calls for me to lie back on a chaise lounge. As I got up I felt dizzy and my heart was pumping like mad. I canceled my next routine, a dance with Vic Damone, and went offstage back to my dressing room.

I knew I had been pushing myself very hard for the past few months, and I didn't like the symptom of a palpitating heart. But I was able to move around, so I walked two blocks back to the Sheraton Hotel and in the lobby I asked the manager if there were a doctor in the house. He panicked, and called the paramedics. They came into my room and strapped me to a bed, while checking a heart monitor. It was all pretty hectic.

Meanwhile, Elliot Kozak, my manager, had gone to a reception after the show—a reception I had been scheduled to attend—and corralled a doctor, who rushed to my room. The doctor pressed hard on the carotid artery in my neck and my heart returned to its normal beat instantly.

The next day I drove down to Cincinnati to do a television show with Bob Braun, and then flew down to Pensacola, where I had promised Jerry Pate I'd play in the pro-am of the Pensacola Open. Jerry lives in Pensacola, and since winning the U.S. Open in 1976 has been one of the top players on the PGA Tour. Colonel Bob Gates had meanwhile lined up a group of doctors from the Eglin Air Force Base near there to look me over, and I was able to play in the pro-am. But it was a scare, and it told me to slow down a little.

In the late summer of 1983, while shaving, I felt a sharp pain behind my right eye. I didn't think too much about it. A few weeks later I flew to England for the Bob Hope British Classic. I had planned to stay in England for another week, but the eye flared up and I took a Concorde to New York to have it checked out by Dr. Bob Ellsworth. The headline in the New York *Post* that day read, BOB HOPE RUSHES TO N.Y. FOR EYE SURGERY, but no surgery was needed. In a few days I was back on the road again.

You can't ignore these warnings, so I watch myself carefully. Nightly rubdowns keep my muscles supple. I get plenty of rest. I haven't smoked in over forty years. I used to love to drink, but several years ago I had a bladder problem that was aggravated by liquor, so I quit drinking.

About that same time I also had a back problem and the doctors were talking about worn-out disks, but my masseur installed a set of exercise rings for me at home and I never heard from my back again.

Dolores deserves a lot of credit for keeping me happy and healthy. She's always been a strong supporter of me as a comedian and as a lover. I only wish she'd learn when to stop laughing.

Eight

Bing

Harry Lillis Crosby. I suppose the mere mention of his name inspires a hundred different reactions, because Bing touched so many people in so many different ways. "Where the Blue of the Night Meets the Gold of the Day." *White Christmas. The Bells of St. Mary's.* The Bing Crosby National Pro-Am at Pebble Beach. His radio and television shows, his movies. Some friends, among them my good pal Phil ("Kinky") Harris, probably remembers Bing best in a duck boat or fishing in a trout stream.

Bing and I made seven "Road" pictures together, but a lot of my fondest memories of him are on a golf course. I really don't know how many rounds we played together around the world—it must have been well over a hundred. He was an excellent player, with the slowest backswing I've ever seen. While he was taking the club back you could fit him for a tailored suit.

I first met him in 1932, at the Friars Club in New York. At that time we were both winding up our careers in vaudeville. We were appearing at the Capitol Theatre, doing three or four shows a day. Bing sang, I was the master of ceremonies. We developed a patter, a little routine that later became the focus for our "Road" movies. Between shows we'd go over to Alex Morrison's driving range under the Fifty-ninth Street bridge and hit golf balls. That was the genesis of a close friendship that endured forty-five years.

Shortly after our booking at the Capitol, Bing went out to Hollywood, where he became a film star. I stayed on Broadway. In 1935 Bing returned for an appearance in New York, and I took him out to Ben Marden's Riviera in Jersey. Harry Richman and Sophie Tucker were in the show. "If you ever decide to come out to California," he told me on the trip back that night, as we were crossing over the George Washington Bridge, "let me know. Maybe we can get together in something."

In 1937 Dolores and I left New York and moved to Hollywood, where I signed with Paramount. Bing was already a big star there. Very large. He was also a prominent member at Lakeside, where he would win the club championship four times. One day Bing asked me over to play. I joined soon after and I'm now an honorary member. Bing introduced me to Maury Luxford, an émigré from New Zealand who was a vital administrative part of Bing's golf tournament for forty years. Maury and Bing shared adjacent lockers at Lakeside. I was already beginning to feel at home in the film capital.

Bing was involved in a horse stable and real estate deals at Del Mar, south of Los Angeles. He invited me down in 1937 for a Saturday night show at the club. We went up on stage and did those routines we had done together five years earlier at the Capitol. Lots of banter and ad-libbing. It went over very well and a Paramount producer, Bill Baron, said, "My God, they're great together. Perfect chemistry. We've got to do something with these boys." That's how the "Road" pictures got started.

Then Bing put me on his Kraft radio show, and when I got my own Pepsodent show on radio, I invited him. Radio was the big thing in those days. The audience was tremendous. Bing had a remarkable ability to double as a straight man or as a comedian. He had a marvelous touch, with exquisite timing. In show business there's a sharp delineation between a comedian and a comic. A comic does broad comedy, with pratfalls and all. A comedian is a line comic—doing lines and stanzas and talking straight to people. Jack Benny, for example, was the consummate comedian. He could take anyone on the stage and make them funny, by his subtle reactions to the audience from a line. Timing. It's all timing. Bing had the same faculty. He could feed a line, and respond to it, and like I say, the chemistry between us was perfect.

And what a golfer! He was always a little better than I was. For a long time his handicap wavered between a 2 and a 4. He worked hard at it. Misery Hill, the practice range at Lakeside, never had a more diligent customer.

He used to practice and play a lot at Wilshire Country Club, too. For a long time I wondered why he'd come to the Paramount lot about nine or ten in the morning with his shoes untied. I'd see him get out of his car and rush into the studio. He'd get up at six in the morning and go out to Wilshire to hit balls for a couple of hours. I was lucky if I could make it to the studio by nine or ten.

Bing actually lived a very quiet existence. He'd go home at night and have a little dinner and be in bed by nine-thirty or ten. Then he'd get up at six and hit balls, or maybe play a few holes with the caddies at Wilshire or Lakeside. Bing was a man who took his golf very seriously.

He may have been the world's worst loser on the golf course. If he was down at the end of 18, he'd suggest playing double or nothing for 3 holes on what he called the "Whisky Route." If he was still down, he'd want to go 3 more, until it got dark. He generally got his money back.

Years ago, in an exhibition before the San Antonio Open, Jimmy Demaret and I beat Bing and Byron Nelson for a $20 nassau. We got busy after the round and nothing was said about the money. A couple of months later I was browsing in the golf shop at Lakeside when suddenly Crosby walked in. He didn't know I was there. Bing asked the pro to change a $100 bill for five twenties. I reached out from behind him, grabbed three of those

Mugging it with Bing on the Paramount lot, several decades ago. I can't remember what I was dressed for but Bing, uncharacteristically, is in western garb. With that driver I'd never fan a tee shot.

bills and said, "Dad, that's for San Antonio." We had a footrace around Lakeside.

There was a golfer playing Lakeside in those days named John ("Mysterious") Montague, who was a shadowy figure. Grantland Rice, who was a Lakeside member, used to write about him. Montague was reluctant to be photographed. Whenever he was in position to break the course record at Lakeside he picked up on the 18th tee. Apparently at one time he had some alleged connections with the underworld, and the word was that he was wanted by the police in Buffalo. He was strong enough to pick up Babe Hardy and hold him upside down. Montague was an excellent golfer, relentless under pressure. We played him for a $5.00 nassau and he'd give you any number of strokes you wanted. He usually won. One day he and Bing had played, and afterward they were sitting around the bar at Lakeside. Bing had lost, and he was a little petulant. "You don't give me enough strokes," he told Montague, and Monty replied, "I can handle you with a shovel, a bat and a rake." So they went out and played one of the most famous 1-hole matches in Lakeside history.

Montague took a bat on the tee and hit a lovely shot. Then he used the same weapon and hit another one, but it veered off into a trap. Bing was on the green in two, about thirty feet from the pin. Montague took his shovel and got the ball on the green. Bing hit his first putt three feet past the hole and Monty said, "That's good, pal," and knocked Bing's ball away. With Bing watching in astonishment, Monty used the rake like a pool cue and knocked the ball right into the cup. Bing shook his head in wonderment, and walked back in.

Bing and I always accused each other of being tight-fisted negotiators in setting up a match. Here's what Bing said about me in Norm Blackburn's historical book on Lakeside: "Bob was usually 30 minutes late on the first tee. In the meantime a crowd would collect and then he'd really do a monologue. He would wiggle around, stall and try to induce you into a match where you couldn't win. It finally got so whenever I'd play with him, I'd just take him for a partner. I'd say, 'I won't play you individually.' We'd just bet the foursome because he'd never make an even game with me. He never lost."

Imagine that! This from my buddy, a man whose pockets were so deep he couldn't have reached them with Montague's rake.

Driver in hand, Bing eavesdrops on a private conversation—a call from E.F. Hutton, naturally—during one of our golf outings at Pine Valley.

But I'll say one thing about Bing—he was never averse to helping me with my game. Once we went over to England to do a picture. We were practicing at Wentworth. They had made us honorary members of the Wentworth Stage and Screen Society of Golfers. I wasn't hitting the ball very well. Bing watched me for a minute or two and then he said, "Just lay back on your right foot a little longer." Man, I started powdering that ball.

In the summer of 1941 Bing and I started playing exhibition matches around the country for the War Relief Fund. The international situation was such that we both felt our country was headed inexorably toward World War II. On December 7, Bing, Dick Gibson and I were staying at Elliott Roosevelt's home in Colorado Springs. When the news came from Pearl Harbor, we decided to join the Navy. Elliott got on the phone with his father in the White House and with Frank Knox, the Secretary of the Navy. Knox wanted to give us commissions in the Navy, but FDR said, "No, we don't want 'em in the Navy. We want 'em to do just what they're doing—entertaining the troops."

That was the origin of our Victory Caravan tours, a series of peripatetic golf matches that actually went on for thirty years and generated millions of dollars in war bond sales and later for the USO. During the war years we did a broadcast at a different military base each week, and tied it in with a golf match.

One day we were playing at George May's Tam O'Shanter Club in Chicago. George was in the business of selling Hawaiian shirts, so we wore them, of course, that day. The gallery was over twenty thousand. They weren't really knowledgeable golf fans, they were motion picture and radio fans, and when we had a shot on the fairway they would just circle around us. I'd say, "Open up, please, we go *that* way."

On about the 3d or 4th tee, as I was addressing my ball, some wag in the crowd yelled, "Hey, Hope, your slip is showing." Everybody laughed. I just looked over and said, "Your father's slip is showing." Bing told that story for years.

From Chicago we went by train to St. Paul, where Wally Mund, the professional at Midland Hills and a national officer in the PGA, had set up an exhibition match at Midland involving himself, Bing, me and Harry Cooper, who was then the golf pro at Golden Valley in suburban Minne-

---

A touch of cranberry juice at the turn during a long-ago round with Bing. On the golf course, Crosby's backswing was so slow I could consume an entire drink before he made contact with the ball.

May 9, 1942, Midland Hills Country Club, St. Paul: Bing, Wally Mund, Harry Cooper, and a shaky yours truly about to tee off in an exhibition. It had been a long night, and I was hardly able to stand up that morning.

apolis. We had a big party the night before at the Radisson Hotel. After about an hour I told Bing I had an invitation to a black-tie party at the Lowry Hotel in St. Paul. So I went over there, had a few drinks and fell asleep about 3 A.M. in a room they had for me.

At nine o'clock the next morning Bing called me. He said, "What are you doing?" I replied, "What do you mean, what am I doing?" Bing said he was on the 1st tee at Midland, and ten thousand people were waiting for us to play. I told him I'd get there as fast as I could.

I jumped into a cab and hurried over to Midland, which is located between Minneapolis and St. Paul. They had a guy waiting there for me with a pair of shoes and a sweater. But now Wally Mund was missing. He had gone looking for me with the Ramsey County sheriff. Wally returned in a few minutes, but he was so shaken he dribbled his shot off the 1st tee. My head was still ringing, but I shot 35 on the front 9. When Wally asked me if I wanted to finish the round, I just said, "Get me a nurse and take me to the first aid room."

Forty-two years later, in the summer of 1984 while I was appearing at the Carlton Celebrity Room near Minneapolis, I went back to Midland and played 9 holes with Wally. He showed me a picture of our foursome on the 1st tee in 1942. I looked a little green around the gills.

At an exhibition in Fort Worth, Bing and I were getting ready to tee off when a guy in the gallery started up his motion picture camera. It sounded like a cement mixer. Bing backed off the ball and remarked, "Why the hell don't you shave at home?"

Bing was a great iron player and took some huge divots. He was also getting bald by this time, and wore a toupee in his movie scenes. One day on the course his caddie, Scorpy Doyle, who is now the starter at Tamarisk in Palm Springs, retrieved one of Bing's jumbo-sized divots, brought it back to him and said, "Try this on for size." Bing chased him for twenty minutes with a brassie in his hand.

When Bing and I were doing *Road to Rio* we heard about a popular soft drink called Lime Cola. It was bottled in Montgomery, Alabama. The guys who founded the company came out to see us about investing in the product. They said they were going to overtake Coca-Cola and become the number one soft drink in the country. Bing and I each invested twenty-five thousand dollars.

We decided to promote the drink in the film. Bing and I each owned one third of *Road to Rio* and Paramount one third, so we installed Lime Cola signs all over the carnival set. Well, before the film was released Lime Cola went under and we had taken a twenty-five-thousand-dollar bath. Every time we went to a preview of that picture, and the Lime Cola signs came on the screen, we reached for the container under the seat.

Bing and I were filming Road to Rio *in 1947 when we took a quick break for a round at Lakeside, with gallery. Bing played a character named Scat Sweeney in the movie and I was Hot Lips Barton. It was our fifth "Road" picture and the one I liked best.*

During my early days in Hollywood, Bing lived right down the street from me on Forman Avenue. Then he moved to Camarillo Street, about six blocks away from my house on Moorpark. One day while we were shooting a "Road" film he heard that his house was on fire. We all raced over to the scene and, sure enough, Bing's house was in flames. Bing pushed a couple of fireman aside and ran through the door of the house into his wardrobe. He came out a few moments later with a shoe in his hand. He reached inside the shoe and took out $2,300 he had hidden in it. Racetrack money.

Once when we were appearing together in Philadelphia he went down and played Pine Valley. I couldn't get away that day. When he came back I asked him how he did. "Oh, great," he said. "I shot 81 on one of the toughest courses in the world." Which it was, and still is. The next day I played there and shot 84. I went into the locker room afterward and the attendant said, "Mr. Hope, would you sign Mr. Crosby's scorecard from his round yesterday?" It was an 84. He had shot an 84, too. Some golfers are that way. They do lie a little.

The oldest course in Palm Springs is O'Donnell, a nice little 9-hole layout. I played it twice one day and shot 66. I told Bing about it and Bing said, "Tsk, Tsk, Bob, I've told you before—you can't walk in after 15. You've got to finish the round."

In our exhibitions around the country Bing always seemed to play a little better than I did. After all, his handicap was a few strokes lower than mine. But I got him every now and then. In 1945 we were playing at the Salt Lake Country Club in Salt Lake City with Ed Dudley and George Schneiter, a couple of smooth-hitting PGA pros. I got off the plane and went to the Utah Hotel to have a chicken sandwich and glass of milk before going over to the course. When the match started I birdied the first 3 holes, nearly making an eagle on the third. Crosby looked at me, with that funny stare of his, and asked, "What are you on?"

Dudley and I were partners. I didn't help him much after the 3d hole but Ed was playing very well and on the 18th tee we were 1-up. Bing was steaming. You know how he liked to win, even in exhibitions. He just plain hated to lose.

Well, on the 18th tee Dudley drove out of bounds and I could see Crosby licking his chops. I hit a commercial drive and managed to hit my second shot safely over a barranca. But the ball was lying on a dandelion patch. I asked Dudley how to play it. "Just hit it like a regular shot," he said. "Forget about the dandelions." I knocked it a foot from the hole to ensure the win for Dudley and me. Crosby chased me down the fairway with a 3-iron.

Bing had originally started his pro-am tournament, at Rancho Santa Fe in 1937, as an outing for his friends in show business and the pros who were playing what then constituted the tour. He liked to tell the story of Sam Snead's presentation ceremony. Sam won the first tournament, which was shortened to 18 holes by rain. Snead had just come out of the mountains of West Virginia and he was really a rustic character. When Bing presented him with the first-place check of $500, Sam stalled a few moments and then said, "If you don't mind, Mr. Crosby, I'd rather have cash."

I played in it for the first time the following year. Bing and I were paired with Snead and Ben Hogan. Snead, who had the mountain man's inbred suspicion of strangers, didn't say a word to me for the first few holes, although he knew who I was. Finally, on about the 5th or 6th tee, he ambled over to me and whispered to me, "Mr. Hope, tell me—how are them Hollywood gals?" Sam was one of us. I always wondered, too.

In 1947, after the war, Bing resumed his tournament on the Monterey Peninsula, and that's where it really took off. I played in it for nearly twenty years, and what great times we had. For the average player, Pebble Beach could be murder. It was Alcatraz with grass. January was not the most clement time of year weather-wise on the peninsula. There were wind and rain and rocks and shrubs and trees and animals, and that was on the greens. I've heard of unplayable lies, but on the tee?

Jimmy Demaret was my pro partner during most of those years at Monterey. Demaret was a marvelous wind player, the best I've ever seen. He was born in a gale down in Texas. His mother had to run five miles to retrieve him.

The 17th hole at Cypress measures 375 yards. In the opening round of the 1952 Crosby, playing into the wind, Jimmy needed a driver, brassie and 4-iron to reach the green, and 1-putted for his par. The wind was swirling in every direction and there were clam shells flying in it.

Demaret shot 70 that day, under impossible conditions, a score that put him pretty well in front. Then Jimmy accompanied Bing and me over to Fort Ord, where Bing did his radio show. While we were rehearsing, Bing got a call from Maury Luxford, the tournament director. Luxford said Mangrum and Middlecoff were wondering when Bing was going to call the round off. Demaret, standing behind Bing, kept saying, "Hey, it's a beautiful day. What are they talking about?" The score stood for that day.

Jimmy won the individual pro division of that tournament, and on the final round he and I were only one stroke off the pro-am lead on the 14th tee at Pebble Beach. The hole is a monster, 555 yards, and we were playing directly into the wind. I hit a good drive and a solid brassie shot. I was pulling out a 4-wood for my third when Demaret came over to see what I was doing.

"Put that club away," he barked at me, and grabbed the brassie out of my bag. I was startled. Here was Jimmy, my old partner in gags, acting like a house detective. He showed me a new grip, so I could fade the shot

An early-vintage Frank Sinatra, the walking 1-iron, vocalizing with Bing. The man at the left doesn't quite know what to make of it. Maybe he'd feel better if his jacket had lapels.

Happy days: Bing and I in one of the early Crosby tournaments, at Rancho Santa Fe in either 1939 or 1940. Judging by the expression on our faces, I'm having the better round.

a little, and said, "Hit it as hard as you can." Well, I hit it hard, and it would up one foot from the cup, for a natural birdie that gave us an eagle with my stroke.

I should say something about the way Bing assigned handicaps at his tournament in those days. His word was final. He would always give the amateurs a stroke or two over their regular handicaps, because the courses we were playing were so tough, and if he liked you he might even add another stroke.

The amateur partner of Art Bell in that tournament was a man named Billy Hoelle. He was a salesman for Minute Maid orange juice. Bing owned a part of that company. On the 18th hole in the final round, Billy Hoelle holed an 8-iron shot from out of the sand along the ocean to tie Bob Toski and Bob Knudson for first place in the pro-am, beating Jimmy and me by one stroke. Bing, ironically enough, claimed he had bought Toski and Knudson in the pro-am.

The parties at the Crosby were legendary. You seldom went to bed. One of the most gracious hosts was Francis Brown, a great player in his younger days who had won the Hawaiian, Japanese and California Amateur championships in the early 1930s. Francis had a beautiful home on a hill at Pebble Beach. I was staying during the tournament with Bing at his home on the 13th hole. We all went over together, including Bing's young son, Linny, who spent the evening talking and eating with the help in the kitchen.

I left the party about 2 A.M. because I had a fairly early starting time. The next morning, at Bing's house, Linny was at the breakfast table with me. I asked him what time he had got home last night and he said four o'clock. "We had *some* time getting back," he said. "When we came around that bend of the road we missed the curve and wound up in the woods." I asked him who was driving, and the boy said, "Dad." I knew that Bing had had a few drinks, so I asked him, "Why did you let him drive?"

Linny said, "He was the best we had."

One year, when I was staying at Francis Brown's house, it snowed on the Saturday night of the tournament. Pebble Beach was covered with a blanket of white. That was the time Jimmy Demaret got off his famous line, "I knew I got loaded last night, but how did I wind up at Squaw Valley?"

Looking out at the snow, I thought, "The hell with this. I'm going home." I got on a Pacific Airlines flight for Burbank and I was sitting on the aisle right behind Jane Wyman, who was sitting across the aisle from her husband, a piano player. The weather was terrible. We got hit by lightning, and I thought the plane had exploded. The pilot came on and announced, "The lightning knocked out our radar. We're going back to San Francisco." Jane and her husband were holding hands over the aisle. I reached up and put my hands on theirs. They looked at me and I said,

The Four Horsemen of the early 1950s at the Crosby: my partner Jimmy Demaret, Jack Burke, and George Coleman. Note the sign plugging Bing's Minute Maid orange juice just behind Jack and George. After playing Pebble Beach you needed antifreeze, not orange juice.

Maury Luxford (left) plays the arbiter while Phil Harris and I haggle over strokes at the Crosby tournament. Maury was the Crosby starter for years, and his introductions on the 1st tee were so elaborate that we often had to hurry to catch up to the group ahead of us.

"You mind if I cut in? I'm alone." I don't know how we ever landed, but we did.

Phil Harris participated in the Crosby for years, usually with a glass in one hand. In his first year, 1951, he won the pro-am with Dutch Harrison. In the last round Phil sank a putt on 17 at Pebble Beach that has been described in length anywhere from seventy-five to ninety feet. When they asked Phil how long it was, he said, "All I know is that I'd love that much footage on Wilshire Boulevard."

Bing and Phil were great pals. They spent a lot of time hunting and fishing together. I've never gone in much for the outdoor-life bit. The fish don't applaud.

It was Bing's friendship with Jimmy Demaret that was responsible for the Legends of Golf, that great senior tournament in Austin, Texas. Bing's daughter Mary Frances went to school for a while in Houston, and whenever Bing would go down to see her, he'd play golf with Demaret. Jimmy was then building the Onion Creek Club in Austin, where they play the Legends. They got to talking about how great it would be to have the seniors play—now this was before the present senior tour; in fact, it actually launched the tour because it proved so popular—and they thought a two-man-team format to be best. Jimmy went to Fred Raphael, who produced "Shell's Wonderful World of Golf" at one time, and the rest is history.

I did a show at the Legends and had a lot of fun. You can't miss with that kind of an audience. "I hear they're filling all the ball washers with Ben-Gay," that sort of thing. "I didn't realize how long some of these seniors have been around. Yesterday I saw a guy signing his scorecard with a feather."

Bing and I had those little bits, those routines with ad-libs. I kidded him about his money and his large family. He needled me about my putting, or anything that came to mind.

In 1957, after he married Kathy Grant and moved up to Hillsborough, just outside of San Francisco, I didn't see him as much. But we did get together in 1961 to film *Road to Hong Kong* in London and we played golf nearly every day at Wentworth. One day, after doing a harem scene, we had the girls giving us manicures. I suggested to the director, Mel Frank, that we have one of the girls give me a pedicure as we were lying on the couches sipping wine. So I had my toes painted as they were shooting the

---

Who's away? Bing, and he hasn't even bothered to tee it up. Yes, the man actually did play with his pipe and hat. Whenever he missed a shot, he could always alibi that his pipe got in the way.

Remember that old game where you matched hands on the bat to determine who was the home team? Bing and I do our own version to resolve honors on the 1st tee, with Professor Jerry Colonna officiating—and also intervening to ward off a typical Crosby ploy.

Bing and I negotiating on the first tee of a match in England, 1975, with Kathy enjoying the dialogue. It was one of our last rounds together.

scene. After we finished I rushed over to Wentworth for a few quick holes. When I had completed 9 holes I was changing clothes in the locker room and I took off my socks. I noticed this fellow across the way looking at me. He noticed my painted toenails. The man looked up in the air and thought for a second: "He couldn't be . . . could he?"

Three weeks later we did the scene where Bing and I had come back from the moon as heroes, and they were throwing confetti on us all day. After the shooting I went over to Wentworth to play. It was hot that day, so I headed for the shower room after the round. There were two Scots toweling off. I took off my shorts, and confetti dropped on the floor. Like I hadn't taken a bath since New Year's. So around Wentworth I was known as the fellow with painted toenails and confetti in my shorts. It added a lot of mystery to my personality.

In October of 1977 a good friend of both Bing and mine, Hugh Davis, dropped dead on the golf course at Baltusrol. I flew East to do a memorial benefit for Hugh at Summit, New Jersey. I was in the Waldorf Towers that afternoon when I got a phone call from Bill Fugazy. Bill told me that Bing had died that day on a golf course in Spain. The shock and the sorrow were so overwhelming I couldn't describe it. I got Alan King to do the show for me in Jersey, and I flew back to California that night. It was a long flight.

I knew that Bing, despite the fact he had still been very active, was not in the best of health. He had lung problems in 1974, which kept him hospitalized during his tournament, and a few years later had that terrible fall off the stage at the Ambassador Theater in Pasadena.

What happened was that as Bing was leaving the stage, at the end of his number, he fell through a hole in the stage and dropped twelve feet. He managed to break the force of the fall by grabbing on to a piece of scenery. I was in my dressing room at the time and when I heard all the commotion I rushed downstairs and he was lying there. Pearl Bailey was holding his head and Kathy was leaning over him. Bing opened his eyes and looked up at me. Then he smiled weakly and said, "Jimmy Dundee couldn't have done it any better." Dundee was our stuntman at Paramount.

Sometime after his death I heard that a doctor in England told him to play only 9 holes because of his heart. Bing had finished 18 that day, and was walking up the hill to the clubhouse, when he collapsed and died.

A part of my life went with Bing. I still miss him and always will, just like the rest of the world. I remember the good times with him, and they'll be with me always.

Nine

Moon Shot

With uncharacteristic immodesty, I must take credit for the inspiration that produced Admiral Alan Shepard's famous golf shot on the moon. Alan got the idea from watching me, enduring a brief moment of crisis, holding a golf club in my hand.

It happened in 1970, while I was doing a television show at NASA with the Apollo group. Shepard and Deke Slayton showed me a training device used by the men who would be soon walking on the moon.

It was a sort of harness for the upper torso, supported by a steel cable. To me it looked like something Mary Martin wore in *Peter Pan*. The apparatus was necessary because of lunar gravity, meaning that on the moon you had only one sixth of your weight on earth.

As I often do, I had carried my driver into the room where they were conducting the tests. Shepard calls it my pacifier. Well, they strapped me into the harness and I, in effect, weighed only one sixth of my normal poundage. Involuntarily I went up on my toes and, feeling just a bit frightened, placed my driver down to act as a tripod.

Shepard, watching closely, had a funny smile on his face. Later he told me that was where he got the idea to take a golf club with him to the moon.

You all know the story of the moon walk. They took off from Houston on January 31, 1971, and on February 5 they landed on the lunar planet. Shepard didn't announce that he was taking a golf club with him, because if anything went wrong he didn't want to be involved with anything as frivolous as hitting a golf ball. But he planned it all very carefully.

Shepard's club was a 6-iron, cut off at the hosel and stuffed into a pocket along with two golf balls. The handle was actually four pieces of aluminum, attached together. When the astronauts had completed all their work on the moon, Shepard thought it was time for his historic shot.

"Because of the cumbersome suit I was wearing, I couldn't make a very good pivot on the swing," he told me. "And I had to hit the ball with just one hand."

Alan was unfamiliar with the course he was playing up there. He had to ask E.T. where the pin was. But I hear E.T. was a great caddie. Every time he went to test the wind, his finger lit up.

The admiral placed two balls in the dust. By his own admission he chili-dipped the first one. "It would normally have gone about thirty yards," he said. "Up there it went two hundred." And landed six inches out of bounds. He shanked the second one—and tossed his club into the Sea of Tranquillity.

No, that's not totally true. He did shank the shot, but he kept that jerry-built 6-iron and today it is displayed in the museum of the U.S. Golf Association at Far Hills, New Jersey.

Shepard started to return to the space ship, but something lying in the dust caught his eye. It was another golf ball, with Jerry Ford's name on it.

This is a special NASA photo of Alan Shepard and his lunarized golf cart on the surface of the moon. He must have been practicing before the photo was made—note the big divot on the right. That must have been some 6-iron.

My day for moon shots may come yet. I have applied to be one of the first civilians into space. When we were working on my TV show in September of 1983 that honored the NASA space program and the astronauts that have been involved, I discovered that starting in 1985 they're going to take civilians along into space.

As I understand it you have to take a six-week test, which I'm sure will be no picnic, that measures physical endurance, emotional stability, courage and whatever else they can come up with. I don't know if I can pass it. But I'm going to try damn hard. How many people have had the opportunity to lay an egg in space?

Maybe Admiral Shepard can use his influence to get me up there. After all, I was the man behind his 6-iron shot on the moon.

There was a man who cost America millions of dollars for a couple of practice shots. His handicap is playing on earth's gravity. Alan has always been so cool and confident. Why not? At the time of his moon shot he was the only astronaut eligible for Medicare.

Shepard was my presenter when Jimmy Demaret and I were inducted into the World Golf Hall of Fame in May of 1983 at Pinehurst, North Carolina. Gene Cernan, another prominent astronaut, did the honors for Jimmy. Then we went out and played 9 holes. I enjoy playing golf with the astronauts. They've helped my scoring—teaching me to count backwards.

Cernan had a good line that day. He looked at Shepard and said, "Here's the man who won the Lunar Open, and his closest competitor was 250,000 miles away."

The Hall of Fame thing was quite an honor. They've got a beautiful building, with all the artifacts, etc., for each inductee. Oddly enough, it was the first time I had ever been to Pinehurst. I couldn't believe it when they notified me. It was almost like inducting John McEnroe into the Diplomatic Hall of Fame. I've done as much for golf as Truman Capote has for sumo wrestling.

But I'm really delighted and proud to be in the World Golf Hall of Fame. I'm generally just happy to be in the fairway. I told them that my plaque shouldn't be in the Hall of Fame building. It should be in the woods . . . about 30 yards out of bounds. Where anyone who wanted to visit my plaque would have to pay a two-stroke penalty.

Shortly before the Pinehurst ceremonies I was honored in the chambers of the U.S. Senate. I was flattered by the invitation. Then I discovered it was authorized by a vote of 50 to 49. Congress had honored me five years earlier. That's a long time to be tied up in committee. I didn't think it was quite fair, though. I'm paying all those taxes and Strom Thurmond is still working on new deductions. But it was really a thrill for a comedian to be honored by his peers.

What made it all the more special for me is that I don't pay any attention to party politics when it comes to friendship. I play golf with Jerry Ford and I play golf with Tip O'Neill, and they both treat me exactly the same. Neither one will let me keep score.

After the ceremonies I did a little sight-seeing. I was having a wonderful tour of the Smithsonian . . . until someone tried to stuff me into a glass case. I wouldn't have minded, but it was Claude Pepper.

Awards do mean a lot to me. In 1983 I received one from a physical fitness foundation in New York. Physical fitness! At my age I consider myself fit just to be breathing. But I do try to work out a little. I go swimming twice a day. It beats buying golf balls.

In 1979 the U.S. Golf Association gave me the Bob Jones Award. The qualities the recipient is supposed to have include, in the official lexicon of the USGA, "respect for the game and its rules, a generosity of spirit, a sense of fair play, self-control and perhaps even self-sacrifice. They are all summed up in the word sportsmanship."

Sportsmanship! Me? A guy whose creative juices flow best when he gets a pencil and scorecard in his hands? I'm glad the USGA didn't monitor what I said under my breath when I missed a shot. that award was very nice, but it ruined about three hundred of my best cheating jokes.

The Metropolitan Golf Writers in New York honored me one year with the Gold Tee Award. That was really a thrill. After all, golf is my real racket. Entertainment is just a sideline.

When I came back to speak at the Gold Tee dinner a few years later I discovered a new comedian, a professional golfer named Peter Jacobsen. This young man is marvelous. He mimicks the mannerisms and speech patterns of his rivals on the tour. He's got it down pat—the violent swing of Arnold Palmer, Johnny Miller with his stiff-armed wave to the gallery, Hubie Green forever hunkered over the ball. But what I liked best was a little skit he did with his pal D. A. Weibring, another pro, who served as Peter's straight man. Weibring portrayed the typically naive sportscaster interviewing Gary Player, played by Peter. Peter had the cap jammed down over his forehead, jaw thrust forward, radiating that bristling defiance of Player. "Gary," Weibring declared, "it's so good to see you again. I know you've been playing all over the world, as usual. What was your last tournament?"

Jacobsen grabbed the mike and with just the right pinch of vindictiveness he loudly declared, "My wife Vivienne and I recently won the Saigon Four-Ball. It was a wonderful world-class event, and I'll tell you this, that's one that Jack Nicklaus has never won."

I loved it so much I told Peter to do his act around the country and he's doing it now, at various clinics and corporate outings. He does a beautiful job.

Admiral Alan Shepard, the moon man, gets a kick out of my own moonmobile at the Desert Classic. Notice that I've got the girl and Shepard's got the backseat.

Peter wasn't even born when I received one of my most treasured awards in golf. In 1942 the PGA gave Bing and myself gold money clips for serving on the organization's Advisory Committee. I still have mine. It gets a lot of use these days when I peel off the bills to pay a nassau bet.

Ten

Gerald Ford: The Man Who Made Golf a Contact Sport

If I were ever backed into a corner and forced to name the people whom I've most enjoyed playing golf with it would, of course, be a difficult task. I've had so much fun on the golf course with so many persons. But very high on any list would be Gerald R. Ford, thirty-eighth President of the United States, genuine good guy and the most dangerous 14-handicapper in the land—in more ways than one.

Jerry Ford's fame as an erratic hitter, capable of beaning anyone within a range of 260 yards, is richly deserved. He's rattled a number of shots off heads and backsides of the fearless followers in his gallery. The President doesn't really have to keep score. He can just look back and count the walking wounded.

I play maybe fifteen or twenty rounds a year with the President, mostly at pro-ams on the PGA Tour including, naturally, the Bob Hope Desert Classic. We also get together at his invitational tournament, which has pros and amateurs, each year at Vail, Colorado. And sometimes we'll just go out and play a social round in Palm Springs, with no gallery except his Secret Service personnel. It's a little different playing with those guys around. I once saw him hit a shot off line and a cactus threw it back onto the fairway.

In the last half dozen years or so President Ford and I have become very close friends. I love the guy. He's so human, so natural. He gets so happy when he hits a good shot or sinks a long putt, and I can tell you that he's pretty good at both. But he's also got a temper, and I've seen him fume after missing a shot.

Ford plays golf with the same fierce determination he showed on the football field for the University of Michigan back in 1932, '33, and '34. He battles you all the way for a $1.00 nassau. He reminds me a lot of Ike in that way. Ford has never shaken one habit of his football days when he played center—he still putts occasionally between his legs.

I've gotten a lot of mileage out of my Jerry Ford jokes. The public enjoys them, because they know that the President does hit a bunch of wild shots, that he loves to play golf as few men do and that he contributes so much to the game. The PGA Tour, in fact, made him an honorary member.

So it's fun to introduce him at dinners with lines like "You all know Jerry Ford—the most dangerous driver since Ben Hur." Ford is easy to spot on the course. He drives the cart with the red cross painted on top.

Whenever I play with him, I usually try to make it a foursome—the President, myself, a paramedic and a faith healer. One of my most prized possessions is the Purple Heart I received for all the golf I've played with him.

But he can play. The President is a considerably longer hitter than I am. I've seen him consistently drive the ball 250 to 260 yards. On the first hole of the Dinah Shore pro-am in 1983, when we were paired with JoAnne Carner, the longest hitter on the women's tour, Carner busted one. She beamed at the gallery's applause and went hoofing down the fairway after her ball. I thought Ford had struck his drive pretty well, too, and when we got out there, Ford's ball was 20 yards out ahead of Carner's. JoAnne couldn't believe it. She said, "Mr. President, that's the longest shot I've ever seen an amateur hit in any pro-am." It was also the straightest he hit that day.

In the Jackie Gleason tournament a few years ago, before one of the largest galleries I've ever seen, Ford was on the green in regulation and putting for birdies on the first 3 holes. He was really happy. Walking over to the 4th tee, I told him, "You know, wouldn't it be funny if you won the U.S. Open?" Ford smiled a little and said, "If I had made one of those birdies I might consider it."

You must remember, however, to be on the alert when you're playing with him. The only safe place is right behind him. He was playing in a charity tournament at Minneapolis in 1974, when he was Vice President, and on the 1st hole he struck a spectator on the head with his drive. Naturally the spectator was standing in the rough. The papers made a big thing out of that.

After all the years of my public needling, Ford is starting to strike back. At banquets he's using lines like "When Bob Hope sings 'Thanks for the Memory,' it reminds him of the last time he broke 90—on a miniature course." Now he's after me for new material he can use on the dais, my jokes about him that he can use on himself.

Every pro-am in the country would love to have him. After all, there are very few unemployed Presidents playing golf. He's a big draw, and the people want to see him. They know what an exciting kind of golf he plays. There's a family living just to the right of the 17th fairway at the Muirfield Village Golf Club in Dublin that has three of Jerry Ford's golf balls. He knocked each of them out of bounds, into that family's backyard, during the pro-ams of the last three Memorial tournaments.

Since he left the White House in 1977 the President has maintained a busy schedule. He's on at least half a dozen corporate boards, and travels all over the country giving speeches. He spends a part of each winter in Vail, Colorado. I played golf with him just the other day and we'd gone 3 holes before he remembered to take off his skis. Ford doesn't really have a lot of time for golf, but he squeezes every minute of it he can, and it's always a red-letter day for any tournament when the President is participating. The galleries idolize him, and for good reason. He's affable, congenial and in every way just a great guy.

Two happy characters at an outing in Cincinnati for the Hope House, one of my favorite charity projects. The President will travel a long way for charity—and also to find his ball.

But he can go the other way, too. When John Curci of the Classic board asked him to play at the opening of Curci's Industry City Hotel in Los Angeles Ford agreed, even though he was troubled by a flare-up of the old knee injury he had suffered playing football at Michigan. During dinner Ford was resting the knee on a chair when a guy walked up and jovially slapped him on the knee. Ford, in deep pain, was furious. "Get your hands off there," he shouted, and I thought he was going to get up and punch the guy in the nose. He probably should have, too.

I don't suppose anyone has ever gotten more free advice about his game from the pros. Nicklaus once spent a couple of long sessions with him, trying to get more acceleration into his downswing. So many times I've seen pros come up to him during a round and say, "Why don't you try this? Move your hands back just a little." Or, "If you'd just open your stance a little, you'll free that left side." They see a lot of the natural athlete in the President and they're anxious to help him improve. But they've never been quite able to curtail that occasional wildness off the tee. Ford is the only man I know who can play four courses simultaneously. There are over fifty courses in Palm Springs, and he never knows which one he'll play until he hits his first drive.

The first time I ever played with him was shortly after he had become President. We had gone over to see Betty in the hospital at Bethesda, Maryland, and then we went out for a round at Burning Tree. He was a fair player at that time, I think about an 18, and he's certainly improved his game since then.

And he's done so much for golf. He's won just about every award there is. The World Golf Hall of Fame, at Pinehurst, North Carolina, owes him a special debt. When the Hall had its opening ceremonies in 1974, on that unforgettable day with the charter inductees honored and a team of parachutists hurtling out of the sky, Ford had just become President. He must have had a million items on his schedule, but he went down to Pinehurst to be with Hogan and Snead and Nicklaus and Palmer and all the stars, and it was his presence that provided the ceremonies with that extra reservoir of prestige.

Shortly afterward I played with the President at Burning Tree. I was staying in the Lincoln Room at the White House, and when I got up the next morning I casually looked through my golf bag. The 6-iron was

Whoa! come back! The Prez wears a horrified look as another of his errant shots heads for the scattering gallery at the Dinah Shore tournament. The only safe place on the golf course with Ford is directly behind him.

To Delores and Bob,
with all our love and
warmest best wishes~ Jerry

missing. I was sure it had wound up in the President's bag, so I called down and asked where he kept his golf clubs. I was told they were in the sporting room.

Well, you've never seen anything like it. I went into that room and there must have been more clubs than in the Spalding plant. It looked like the bag storage room at the U.S. Open. I spotted his bag and there was my missing 6-iron. I don't know why he would have wanted it—it never hurt anybody.

I was ready for Gerald Ford's golf game because I had played many rounds several years earlier with Spiro Agnew when he was Vice President. Now there was a real wild man on the golf course. When Agnew yelled "Fore!" you never knew whether he was telling someone to get out of the way or if he was predicting how many spectators he would hit with the shot.

Actually it was exciting playing golf with Agnew. You never had to wait for the group ahead. They were all hiding in the bushes. I was his partner one day at Palm Springs, although I didn't realize it until my caddie handed me a blindfold and a cigarette.

A couple of weeks later we were playing again. There was a foursome of nuns behind us. The sisters must have heard all about Agnew, because they asked if they could pray through.

Then Ford came along and I became not only a friend but one of the survivors. I think Ford could have made it in show business . . . as anything but a knife thrower. But I enjoy playing with him. That element of risk gets my adrenaline flowing and adds twenty yards to my tee shots. You don't know what fear is until you hear Ford behind you shouting "Fore!" . . . and you're still in the locker room.

One day Ford asked me what term I used when conferring with Dwight Eisenhower.

"He wanted his friends to call him Ike," I said. "So I did."

"What did he call you?"

"He always called me . . . well, you know how upset you can get when somebody talks on your backswing."

Shortly after I started playing golf with Jerry Ford I thought it was time to take some lessons. Not golf lessons. First aid. But you know, the

---

One of my favorite shots. The Fords and the Hopes having dinner together at my home in Palm Springs. We've shared a lot of meals over the past several years, every one a joy. By the way, note how debonair and handsome we all look. It must have been Dolores' cooking.

The Prez and I applauding a shot to the green by one of our playing partners at the Desert Classic. Note his inscription at the lower left: "with appropriate financial support." That's really hitting below the belt.

President has improved his game and now he plays at a golf club in Palm Springs that is so exclusive that the ball washer has a wine steward.

In 1977, playing in the pro-am of the Danny Thomas Memphis Classic, Ford got a hole in one. It made page-one news all over the country the next day. Danny allows one miracle there every year. But right after the ace, Ford returned to his old self. He took the ball out of the cup, threw it to the gallery and missed.

Whenever I play with Ford these days I carry thirteen clubs and a white flag. I try to win only enough from him to pay my extra insurance premiums. In one round at Eldorado in Palm Springs the gallery ended up with more dimples than his golf ball had.

But I jest. He's really a fine trap player. He seldom misses one. He drives well, too. He's never lost a golf cart yet.

One reason the Bob Hope British Classic drew such big galleries was that Ford went over and played in the pro-am the last three years. They love him in England just like they do in America.

At the pro-am dinner the first year he was there I told the British audience I wasn't sure how to describe his golf game. He's to golf what Prince Charles is to steeplechase riding. I guaranteed them one thing: Gerald Ford would put their National Health program to the test. And then I gave them a little tip—Ford's second shot is the one to watch. It means you survived his first.

Actually Ford had been in England on several previous occasions, but never for golf. The other trips were all peacetime visits. The Americans know he's a dangerous golfer because they chipped in to send him over.

My tournament in England was the first time Ford was allowed to play golf on foreign soil. We found a loophole in the SALT agreement. He played British golf on the 2d hole. Two spectators got stiff upper lips. On the 3d hole his caddie enlisted for service in Northern Ireland. He wanted at least a fighting chance. Why not? In America his Secret Service men are demanding combat pay.

We had great weather over there, but one day it got a bit British and I wore a thermal vest, wool shirt, three sweaters and a windbreaker. Ford was laughing because I finished my follow-through before my clothes had started my backswing. Big deal. On the 18th tee Ford put a ball through the clubhouse window. It wasn't easy. It was behind him. That's when I remembered that the Russians used to say if we were really serious about disarmament, we'd dismantle his golf clubs.

But what a great guy. He watched the 1981 U.S. Amateur finals on television and when Nathaniel Crosby won he called me, really bubbling with excitement. "It wasn't just his putting, Bob," he said. "That young man hit a lot of greens with his iron shots."

I had to agree. There hasn't been a Crosby with that much accuracy since Nathaniel's sister Mary Frances shot J. R. Ewing.

Knickers returned to the American golf scene in the early 1980s, and here are the Prez and myself in our natty plus fours at the Desert Classic in '82.

Ford was at Pebble Beach on the last round of the 1982 U.S. Open, when Tom Watson beat Jack Nicklaus by chipping in for a birdie on the 17th hole. The President and I got together the next day and he couldn't stop talking about that shot.

"Listen," I told him, "that ball traveled only twenty-seven feet. I hit a lot of shots twenty-seven feet. Sometimes with my driver."

"Yes, but do you realize the ball went twenty-seven feet and never hit anybody?"

Reminiscing about Jerry Ford reminds me that I've had the pleasure of playing golf with six Presidents—Ford, Ike, John Kennedy, Lyndon Johnson, Richard Nixon and Ronald Reagan. Reagan doesn't play much anymore, but he once broke 100 and that's pretty good for a man on horseback.

Kennedy could have been an outstanding player, bad back and all. He was an excellent striker of the ball. I don't think golf appealed all that much to JFK. He often appeared restless and detached on the course. I guess sailing and touch football were his games.

Another President who took his golf casually was LBJ. I played with him only once, in Acapulco. Darrell Royal, who was then the Texas football coach, played with us. I think LBJ enjoyed getting out that day, but he didn't seem to have much touch or feel for the game.

Nixon was a different matter. He played with a lot of gusto and enthusiasm, favoring the down-the-middle approach. Nixon never had the natural athletic instincts of Kennedy or Ford, but he got his game down to a 14-handicap and he took his rounds seriously.

I'll never forget the time Nixon came out to play Lakeside, and I don't suppose George Gobel, or his wife Alice, will, either. Nixon was in the White House at the time. I was talking to him one day and he said he was coming out to California. I asked him to play with me at Lakeside. I suggested a foursome. He said, "Good, get Jimmy Stewart and Fred MacMurray to round it out." So I did.

The President's security people arrived at my home at 10 A.M. in a helicopter, buzzing in over the hedge surrounding the house. The neighbors thought it was a delivery from Chicken Delight. Nixon came two hours later, with Bebe Rebozo. We took them over to Lakeside. Nixon acted like he was campaigning, hugging and kissing everyone in sight. I told him, "Mr. President, you're already elected." I thought it was pretty funny, but I didn't notice him laughing.

After the round we adjourned to the locker room. Gobel was there and so was Norm Blackburn, the Lakeside historian. Gobel passed by my locker and I said, "George, come here and meet the President." Nixon said, "Sit down and have a drink with us." Gobel replied, "I'd like to, but I'm supposed to meet Alice pretty soon. She'll never believe I was having a drink with the President of the United States."

A rare photo indeed: I'm studying President Nixon's swing mechanics in the Oval Room of the White House, 1973.

Nose to nose with Richard Nixon during his White House years. I'd have to say the contest was about a draw.

Nixon laughed and said, "Well, go call Alice and I'll speak to her and explain it."

Knowing Alice and her freewheeling personality, we all held our breath. But they appeared to be having a nice conversation and then the President said, "You know, Alice, George will probably be a little late tonight." She said, "Oh, that's all right, I'm used to that."

Then Nixon told her, "I almost had a hole in one today. It was a brand-new ball and it's got my name on it. I'm going to wrap it up and have George take it home to you."

It was a nice thing for the President to do, and with that we all sat down and had another round of drinks.

I've always enjoyed playing golf with a President. The only problem is that there are so many Secret Service men around there's not much chance to cheat.

Eleven

The Desert Classic:
Pigeons in Palm Springs

Every year shortly after Christmas I start to get ready for one of my pet projects, the Bob Hope Desert Classic. It's held in January in Palm Springs, and I'm happy to say it's one of the most popular events on the PGA Tour. Of course Palm Springs is such a great place to play golf. It's the only place I know with lawn chairs in the sand traps.

The Classic has the largest field of any event on the pro tour—136 pros and 408 amateurs. The competition is held over four desert courses. Bermuda Dunes, Indian Wells and La Quinta are annual sites; Eldorado and Tamarisk alternate each year.

Our format is a little different from most tour events in that we go 90 holes instead of 72. The amateurs are drawn for three-man teams early in the week and they stay together for four days, Wednesday through Saturday, playing with a different pro each day. On Sunday the pros go at it alone for the money.

Speaking of money, it takes a little to play in the Classic. The entry fee is $3,600 for each amateur who is not a member of any of the five participating clubs and $2,000 apiece for host club members. It's actually a good deal. The boys get four days of great competition on those lovely courses in beautiful weather—it's beautiful most of the time, anyway—and they get a rare opportunity to rub noses with the biggest names on the pro circuit. They also receive a gift bag full of so many nice things that sometimes I wonder how we can make any money on the tournament.

But we do manage to turn a handsome profit and it all goes to charity. The Eisenhower Medical Center gets 70 percent of the proceeds and the other 30 percent is divided among 39 charities in the Coachella Valley. The Classic has raised over $10 million for the Eisenhower center.

We have many, many more applications for berths from amateurs than we can possibly accommodate. Selecting the field is a difficult task, ably done by our board of directors. My only real contribution is to pick eighteen or twenty celebrity contestants who donate their time and effort to help make the Classic the truly important and fun event that it is.

Many of the amateurs help fill the coffers with donations of up to $5,000, over and above their entry fees, to our charity recipients. This is one reason that in recent years we have been able to raise an average of $1 million a year for the charities.

I used to play in the first four rounds each year, but lately I've cut that back to playing in the opening round on Wednesday and again on Saturday. After the Saturday round I hustle up to the NBC tower to provide television commentary, and on Sundays I put in a full shift with the TV crew.

One of our star attractions is my friend Gerald Ford, who has been a contestant since 1977. That year I asked him if he'd like to play, thinking he'd probably do just one round, but he asked me, "Do you mind if I play every day?" He usually has the largest gallery of the tournament. It's great to have Tip O'Neill in every year, too. On hot days he supplies a lot of shade.

Tournament week begins on Monday night with the Classic Ball, a black-tie extravaganza with a thousand guests, held at the Hilton Riviera in downtown Palm Springs. It's a terrific fund-raiser for our charities, with fifty sponsors contributing $5,000 apiece. I do a show with a lot of help from pals like Glen Campbell, Andy Williams, Charley Pride, Danny Thomas, Phyllis Diller, Sammy Davis, Jr., and other top-line entertainers.

In 1971 we invited King Hassan of Morocco, one of the most fanatical golfers I've ever known, over to play in the Classic. The King couldn't make it, but he sent one of his most trusted advisers, a General Medbouh. The general and his wife attended the ball and posed for several pictures with various guests. I remember it particularly well, because I was in one of the photos.

The general mentioned that King Hassan was interested in establishing a tournament in Morocco that would be patterned after the Desert Classic. Robert Trent Jones had designed a course near Rabat. A couple of months later there was an invitation from General Medbouh for General Bill Yancey, who was then our tournament's executive director, to come to Morocco in July for ceremonies that would include a celebration of the King's birthday and the opening of the golf course. Bill had come aboard in 1966 after his retirement from the Air Force.

Yancey was staying at the King's palace along with Trent Jones and Claude Harmon, the 1948 Masters champion and longtime pro at Winged Foot, who had become a close friend of the King. Billy Casper, another friend of the King, was due in the following day.

Yancey had just finished his lunch when he decided to stroll out on the balcony for a look at the countryside below. He heard a series of sharp noises that sounded to him like firecrackers. He wasn't alarmed at all, because he had lived for a time in China, where firecrackers are a vital part of any celebration.

Suddenly there were live bullets whining and people falling. Blood was flowing everywhere. The palace was under siege, in a revolt staged by a military group intent on taking over the country. Who do you think was leading that revolt? None other than our old friend General Medbouh.

Yancey and his group were held prisoners at gunpoint for over four hours. People were shouting orders at him in a language he didn't understand. When the King was brought out, his hands tied, and pushed to the floor in front of Yancey, Bill figured that was it. They were going to shoot the King and every other prisoner in the building.

General Medbouh himself was shot and killed that afternoon, by one of his own men. It turned out later that his part in the uprising was somewhat ambiguous, that he was actually trying to help the King. But nobody is

Tip O'Neill, my favorite foursome, with President Ford and Lee Trevino at the Desert Classic. Tip plays in the Classic every year and I always try to be paired with him because on a hot day you're guaranteed plenty of shade.

The calm before the storm. General Medbouh and his wife (seated) and Brigadier General William Yancey at the Classic Ball, February 1971.

really sure today just what his role was. The revolt was quelled later in the day and the King, together with Yancey, Jones, Harmon and others, was released. I don't think they played the course that day.

Yancey survived, and continued as our executive secretary until 1982, when he resigned and was replaced by Ed Heoreodt, a retired executive with Chrysler. Yancey did a marvelous job for us, and his efforts are being ably continued by Heoreodt and our press director, Cliff Brown, who was with us from the start. Heoreodt and Brown work closely with our board of directors in keeping things running smoothly throughout the year.

The Classic had its origins in the old Thunderbird Invitational, a $5,000, 36-hole pro-am instituted in 1952 at the Thunderbird Ranch and Country Club. I played in it, along with Phil Harris, Randolph Scott, Hoagy Carmichael, Ralph Kiner and pros like Jerry Barber, Jackie Burke, Jimmy Demaret, Dutch Harrison, Lawson Little, Lloyd Mangrum, Cary Middlecoff, Johnny Revolta, Jimmy Thomson and Lew Worsham. It was the first appearance of professional golfers in the Palm Springs area.

In 1960 it became the Palm Springs Golf Classic, a $100,000 event with 90 holes of competition over five days at Tamarisk, Thunderbird, Indian Wells and Bermuda Dunes. Arnold Palmer, who would go on to claim five Classic titles, won the first one and his check was $12,000, which would hardly cover tip money today. The biggest bonanza went to Joe Campbell, the cigar-chewing pro from Purdue who walked off with $50,000 for scoring a hole in one, on the 205-yard 5th at Tamarisk.

Jack Nicklaus won it for the first time in 1963 in a play-off with Gary Player. The next year my old Crosby partner, Jimmy Demaret, made a valiant run before missing a couple of short putts and losing in a play-off to Tommy Jacobs. Jimmy, well into his fifties then, told me later it was the most heartbreaking loss of his career.

In the early 1960s Ernie Dunlevie, the founder of Bermuda Dunes, and the late Milt Hicks, who was president of Indian Wells, asked me to take over the Classic, but I really didn't have the time and I had to decline. Dunlevie and Hicks didn't give up that easily. Next they asked me to help find a corporate sponsor. I approached Chrysler and they said fine, if I'd put my name on it. So in 1965 the Bob Hope Desert Classic was born, maintaining the same 90-hole format.

Billy Casper won it with a four-foot birdie putt on the final hole at Bermuda Dunes to hold off the charging Palmer, setting a precedent in which every year the finish seems to boil down to one last putt. There hasn't been that much excitement on TV since a giant salmon tried to take Merlin Olsen upstream.

The fans swarmed out to watch the pros and the celebrities. The freeway was bumper to bumper . . . with golf carts. Palm Springs is a great golf town. They won't let you in unless you're wearing an alpaca sweater. It's the only place in the world where the gophers wear crash helmets. And the Classic is the only event in the world where guys can get money out of a desert without drilling for oil.

One day the greens were all torn up and we found out why. It was an accident. Ike was wearing his army boots.

In 1966 Doug Sanders beat Palmer in a play-off after Palmer had birdied the 90th hole to tie, but Sanders was the victim the following year when he missed a birdie putt on the final hole and Tom Nieporte won. Nieporte's wife was expecting their eighth child at the time, so instead of awarding him the customary Chrysler car as a supplementary prize we presented Tom with a station wagon that he had requested.

Moon Mullins has a page in Classic history, too. Moon, who was the pro at Indian Wells, broke the competitive course record at La Quinta with a 65 on the second round in 1970. On the final round, also at La Quinta, poor Moon shot 82.

Palmer won his fifth Classic in 1973, in a memorable showdown with Nicklaus at Bermuda Dunes. They were paired together on a rainy day in the final round. On the last hole Nicklaus could have tied with an eagle putt from thirty feet. Palmer watched nervously as Jack stroked the ball. It just missed the cup. At the presentation ceremonies Palmer nudged Jack and said, "Hey, what were you trying to do to me out there?" Nicklaus looked him in the eye and replied, "Why, Arnold, I was trying to beat you." The gallery got a kick out of that.

The NBC television cameras caught the crestfallen look on Rex Caldwell's face on the 90th hole in 1983, when Keith Fergus rolled in a twenty-footer to tie him and then beat Rex on the first play-off hole. Caldwell went on to lose another play-off the next week at Phoenix.

So many zany things have happened at the Classic. A few years ago Gary Hallberg played his approach shot to the green from the clubhouse roof at Indian Wells. Gary's second shot had struck a cart path behind the green and bounced up on the roof. He could have taken a free drop, but from where the drop would be made he had no shot to the green. So we got a ladder and he climbed up to the roof and hit the ball with his wedge. Amazingly enough, he made the putt for a par.

Spiro Agnew was one of our featured attractions during his days as Vice President. He was one of the wildest shotmakers I've ever seen. He sprayed his shots everywhere. In 1970 he conked his pro partner, Doug Sanders, on the head with a drive and nailed three spectators with other shots during a single round at Bermuda Dunes. Agnew was our Veep, after all, so I guess he was entitled to a few wild shots.

One year we had to hold the tournament over a day because a flash flood had isolated several holes on the back 9 at Indian Wells. Johnny Weissmuller was the only golfer who could have played those holes.

Ike with a collection of hams at the 1968 Desert Classic. Left to right: Toney Penna, the master clubmaker; Ed Crowley, who managed big hotels for as long as I can remember and played in all the major golf tournaments; Doug Sanders, in subdued hues for him; Tom Nieporte, the quiet champion and our boy Pat Boone. It was Ike's last year at the Classic and one we'll all remember.

A radiant Arnold Palmer at the NBC mike, the Desert Classic trophy in front of him, after defeating a crew-cut Deane Beman in a play-off for the 1968 Desert Classic title. Ike's at the left, several of our tournament committeemen in the background and a future President named Reagan is at the right.

With Dolores looking on, Ike exchanges golf gossip with Ray Bolger during the 1968 Desert Classic. It must have been a cool day: Ike's wearing a sweater underneath his jacket, Bolger has a turtleneck and sweater and Dolores is wearing gloves. In Palm Springs?

A time for reflection . . . and testing the water on the 18th at Indian Wells with my bare foot. Milt Harper took this memorable shot in 1978. That's President Ford and Pete Sesso, a tour rules official, right behind me and Tom Watson off to the left. P.S.—I picked up and dropped.

In a festive moment at the conclusion of the 1982 Desert Classic. Ed Fiori and Tom Kite, surrounding President Ford, had just come in from their sudden-death play-off that Fiori (left) won with a putt from here to Zanzibar.

A happy Bruce Lietzke, who had just set the Desert Classic record of 335 in 1981, flashes his $50,000 check behind the Eisenhower Trophy, with President Ford and runner-up Jerry Pate looking on. With a score like that, I had to ask Bruce whether he had played all 90 holes. I've shot 335, too, but it took me only a weekend to do it.

That's right, 32 under! Our Gang is going great guns at the Desert Classic. Lee Trevino, at 6 under, did his share (that's Trevino's caddie, Herman Mitchell, behind his right shoulder). Lee looks serious, but to a couple of veteran campaigners like the Prez and myself, it's a piece of cake.

Players occasionally have to contend with those gusty desert winds. I hit a ball into the wind one day at La Quinta, but I guess I shouldn't have watched it with my mouth open. I'm the only guy around with an Adam's apple marked SPALDING TOP-FLITE.

People ask me why at my age I still play in the Classic. I have to. I'm at an awkward age—too old for marbles and too married for women.

One of the most rewarding spin-offs from our tournament has been the creation of the Bob Hope British Classic. I guess the origins of the British Classic date back to 1961, when Bing and I were in England filming *Road to Hong Kong* with Joan Collins. Herbert Morrison, former Deputy Prime Minister, came over to the set one day and said, "Why don't you come over to Royal Blackheath and see your golf course?" I didn't know what he meant, but I went along.

Royal Blackheath, once a Roman battleground, is located in the village of Eltham, about a block or two from where I was born on May 29, 1903, at 44 Craighton Road. The visit with Herbert Morrison motivated me to do something for my hometown. I decided I wanted to build a theater. The British Classic turned out to be an ideal vehicle for fund-raising, so we launched it in 1980 with a field of top American and British pros, leading British amateurs and a delegation of my pals from show business in Hollywood.

We lost money the first year and broke about even in the second. In 1982 the tournament really caught on, with celebrity attractions like Gerald Ford, Jim Garner, Telly Savalas and others, and golfers such as Lee Trevino, Steve Ballesteros and Sam Snead. And the theater in Eltham was built.

Just as Herbert Morrison was the spark behind the Bob Hope British Classic, the man behind the founding of the Eisenhower Medical Center was the late Freeman Gosden, of "Amos 'n' Andy," who was a close friend of Ike. Freeman was always pushing me to get the center built. I thought it was a good idea, too.

The obvious location for it was where it stands today, on what was then called Del Sol Road in Palm Springs. I owned some land in that area, and to tell you the truth I was waiting for the committee that had been formed to approach me about that land. What happened was that I gave eighty acres for the center, and that's when they renamed the road Bob Hope Drive. Ground was broken for the center in 1969.

My wife Dolores was president of the Eisenhower Medical Center for seven years, and later became chairman. Freeman Gosden and others like

---

The Hopemobile, the ultimate in comfort for the golfer. We unveiled it a few years ago at the Desert Classic. Any resemblance to its namesake is purely intentional.

Here I'm getting double-bussed at the Desert Classic by one of our hostesses and Irene Ryan, a delightful character who gave us so many laughs on "The Beverly Hillbillies."

Gus Levy (chairman of the finance committee), George Champion and George Love were instrumental in staging a fund-raising dinner in New York, which generated $1,850,000.

Love, the founder of the Laurel Valley Golf Club near Pittsburgh, had gone out on a snowy day in Pittsburgh to line up donors for the dinner. I've always been grateful to him for that.

It was just about the most impressive dais I've ever seen at any dinner. Mamie was there. So were Bing, Cardinal Cooke, Governor Rockefeller, Ray Bolger, Johnny Cash, Arnold Palmer, Oleg Cassini, Raquel Welch, Neil Armstrong and a host of other celebrities. That's what really got the center rolling, and later Walter Annenberg set up another big fund-raising dinner in Los Angeles.

When we dedicated the Eisenhower Medical Center, on November 27, 1971, Ike was gone. He had died on March 28, 1969. But Mamie was on hand for the ceremonies, along with President Nixon, Vice President Agnew and a governor of California by the name of Ronald Reagan. As we were touring the hospital, Reagan told me, "I can't believe you did this without any government money." But we did, and to me it will always be the most lasting legacy of the Desert Classic.

I think of this every time Dolores and I drive past the center, with all its wonderful facilities that do so much good for so many. And more important, the center, now a large community, is in the black and growing each year.

The Probst Professional Building was the first to be dedicated, followed by the Kiewit Building, the Wright Building, the Annenberg Center, the Hal Wallis Research Center, the Betty Ford Center and the Eisenhower Memorial Hospital with its Ike and Mamie wings. The most recent addition was the Gene Autry Tower, named in honor of the former movie cowboy, baseball club owner and longtime Palm Springs philanthropist who donated $5 million to the hospital. I've been rooting for Autry's team, the California Angels, ever since.

I tip my hat to all the people connected with the Classic and the center who have worked so hard on behalf of the center and all the desert charities—John Sinn, John Curci, Paul Jenkins, Walter Probst, Peter Kiewit, Kenneth Baldwin, Joseph Cannel, Curly Simon, Ernie Dunlevie, Willard Keith, Cliff Brown, Al Sedgwick, Bob Miller, Ralph Dutro, Gordon Metcalf, Jim Aiken, Bill Garland, Saul Kamin, Leonard Krieger, Victor LoBue, Bob Manning, Lou Souza, Raymond Kaiser, Jack Clark, Paul Wierk, Joe Checkers, Robert and Honor Barit, Gerald Ford, and my two dancing partners, Alex Spanos and Betty Ford.

Then I think of all the celebrities who have donated so much of their time and talent to the cause—Tip O'Neill, Telly Savalas, Alex Spanos, Buddy Rogers, Jack Lemmon, Andy Williams, Glen Campbell, Alan

Shepard, Neil Armstrong, Scatman Crothers, Bob Goulet, Lawrence Welk, Foster Brooks, Gordon MacRae, Charley Pride, Fred MacMurray, Efrem Zimbalist, Sammy Davis, Jr., Clint Eastwood, Flip Wilson, Congressmen Dan Rostenkowski, Bob Michel, and Marty Russo, and Joey Bishop. (One night at the Classic Ball we had thirteen comedians on the card, Bishop being the final one, and he came onstage, leered at me and cracked, "So you thought you needed another comedian?")

Ronald Reagan has been there a couple of times, Ike was there in the 1960s and Gerald Ford every year. I'm also indebted to the pros who show up, year after year, at a time so early in the season when they would probably rather be home with their families. It's been a very satisfying endeavor for all of us.

My only regret is that they don't have an intensive care unit in the Eisenhower Medical Center for my golf game.

Twelve

Have Clubs, Will Travel

Golf is an international game. After all, it started in Europe several centuries ago, and didn't catch on in the United States until the 1890s. I've played all over the world, which means there probably isn't a country with a course in which I haven't 3-putted.

One of the trips I remember most fondly was my lone appearance in the British Amateur. It was 1951, May 21—26, at the Royal Porthcawl course in Wales. I got beat in the first round by a man smoking a pipe, which of course delighted Crosby.

I'd been thinking about playing in the British Amateur for around a year before that. Thanks to my lessons from Ben Hogan and some helpful tips from other pros, I was playing the best golf of my life at that time. My handicap was 6. I worked hard on my game for several months, and by the time I mailed my entry I was down to a 4.

Bing had played in the British Amateur in 1950, at St. Andrews, and came home raving about it. He lost his first match, but he had a huge gallery and birdied the opening hole. "You're playing well enough to take a crack at it," he told me. "You owe it to yourself to enter." Joe Dey, who was then executive director of the United States Golf Association, told me I would enjoy it, so I packed up and took off.

The first leg of the trip involved doing some shows for our servicemen in Germany, then I flew to Scotland for a round at St. Andrews and headed over to Wales. I was invited by Dick Berlin, who worked for William Randolph Hearst, to stay at St. Donat's Castle, six miles from Cardiff. There were thirty-six suites in the castle and I was the only one there. I felt like Christine Onassis.

Several of my American golfing friends, among them George Coleman, Francis H. I. Brown, Eddie Lowery and Hobart Manley, were also entered in the British Amateur. I was ready for my debut in a national championship.

My opponent in the first round of match play was a paint salesman from Yorkshire named Charlie Fox. Charlie was at Porthcawl on a little vacation with his wife Muriel. I watched him on the practice tee and thought, "I can beat this guy at Lakeside."

Charlie Fox smoked a pipe throughout the round and wore glasses that looked like the bottom side of a scotch bottle. Once he got near the green he used a 7-iron on every shot and, as I was to painfully discover, it was his magic wand.

I got off to a shaky start, hitting my first drive into the rough and topping two shots on the 2d hole. On the 5th I hit one over a fence and on the 9th I got into one of those huge bunkers. At the turn I was 3 down.

We had a gallery of over a thousand. Most of the fans were pulling for me, and I really don't think Charlie himself would have minded if I won. He suggested a drop out of a bush for me on one hole in a more favorable spot than I would have placed it.

The British Amateur, Royal Porthcawl, 1951. What a classic swing! It's obvious that the gallery is impressed. I only wish my opponent had been. I lost my first match.

By the 12th or 13th hole I was playing pretty well but Charlie was getting it up and down with that 7-iron and a hot putter and he finally closed me out 2 and 1. I headed for the bar, and there were Francis Brown, who had lost his match 8 and 6; Hobart Manley, who had gone down 3 and 1; and our two winners, George Coleman and Eddie Lowery. George got nailed 6 and 5 by Charley Coe in the second round but Lowery advanced to the third round before he lost.

After a few drinks at the bar we all headed to my castle for more drinks. Hearst had a $2 million collection of armor, worn by the knights of old. After several more pops we each put on a suit of armor and pretended we were Douglas Fairbanks, Sr. What a scene that was. The Hearst servants stood around in amazement.

America had a particularly strong delegation of golfers in that tournament. Outstanding players like Dick Chapman, Charley Coe, Frank Stranahan, Sammy Urzetta, Bill Ebert, Bill Campbell in addition to Lowery and Coleman. Chapman beat the great Irish star Joe Carr in the semifinals and then whipped Coe 5 and 4 in the finals.

It was cold and rainy the day I played at Porthcawl, but that was nothing compared to the conditions I've encountered elsewhere around the world. In Australia the winds nearly blew us off the golf course. In Korea there was a foot of snow on the ground, but the army engineers cleared a fairway and green for me and I played 9 holes.

Alaska was cold, too, and you could play until eleven o'clock at night. One course in Alaska was hacked out of the wilderness. My caddie was a moose. Every time I reached for a club he thought I was trying to steal his antlers.

In Casablanca they had a beautiful course, seven thousand yards of sand. Every once in a while there was a little patch of grass. That was a trap.

Okinawa had a lovely course. You're really in trouble in a bunker because nobody remembers where the Japanese buried their land mines. You can miss the ball completely and blast out.

It won't be long before golf is as popular in China as it is in Japan. Arnold Palmer is building a course there now, and you can be sure several others will be popping up. When I was in China the only course was one that the British had built in Shanghai, but that's gone now.

I took my clubs with me to China, hoping to hit some balls here and there. In Peking I walked down the street with my driver. Nobody looked at me. They looked at my golf club. They thought it was a bomb. The Chinese people didn't know me, but one night when I was out walking, a Chinaman who had been raised in America came up and said, "Bob Hope, what are you doing here?" He was drinking a Coke.

It looks like Scotland in the background, but it's the Lakes Golf Club in Sydney, Australia, 1955. Everyone looks sopping wet, including the tiger with the abbreviated swing.

On one trip I was staying on an aircraft carrier in the China Sea. We did a show on the ship at night, and the next morning the captain, who was a golfer, came up to me with a big bag of balls. He had arranged to have several destroyers lined up about two hundred yards away, so we teed them up on the carrier and tried to knock them across the water onto the destroyers.

We played all over the South Pacific. At Christmas Island they had sand crabs that walked sideways. It was the damndest thing I ever saw.

Golf's really fun in Japan because of the women caddies. They're gorgeous. It was the first time I ever saw a pro kiss his caddie. I saw one guy start out playing alone with his caddie. By the 9th hole they were engaged and when they finished on 18 they had a foursome.

We had a few Japanese women caddies one year at the Desert Classic. It was Ernie Dunlevie's idea. The pros were told they were to be returned at the end of the tournament—no taking home souvenirs.

I had a Japanese caddie at the Classic and on one hole she smiled and handed me a hara-kiri sword. I smiled, and shanked that, too.

There was one round in Hawaii I'll never forget. It took forever to play the first 9. I couldn't understand it. They sent a marshal out to locate the reason and he found it on the 11th hole. A foursome of Japanese men were playing, using just one ball for the group. One guy would hit, and another would rush out to mark the ball. Then he'd bring it back and the second man would tee off with the same ball. They had the whole town backed up. And that's a true story.

I take my golf clubs with me all over the world. It's amazing what you can get through customs in a golf bag.

Ward Grant, one of my public relations people, did a little research on the subject recently and concluded that I've played about two thousand courses. Some of them would hardly qualify for the Open Championship, but they had tees, fairways, greens and flags. Lord knows on how many of those two thousand courses there was a pro who tried to help me with my game. I've gotten bootleg lessons from Brazil to Bangkok.

When I think of all those rounds and all those matches in England, Scotland, France, Germany, Spain, Morocco, Thailand, Japan, Korea, Australia . . . I've left more money overseas than Congress.

The caddies in Scotland are something else. If you hit a bad shot they sneer at you. They all sound like Rickles with a burr. And they dress so nicely. Scotland has the only pro shops that sell cummberbunds.

I did shows for our troops in Vietnam for nine years. The government wouldn't let us stay in Saigon, because they felt it was too dangerous. The Cong had made a pledge to wipe out our entourage. So we stayed in Bangkok, at the Erawan Hotel, and flew each day into Vietnam for the shows.

Mid-season form on the deck of the carrier Ticonderoga *in the China Sea, 1965. I never had to worry about a bad lie.*

Once in a while we got a day off and I spent it playing golf at the Sporting Club in Bangkok. It was nearly as hazardous as Saigon. The course had crisscrossing fairways and I wasn't far away when a friend of mine, Colonel Gates, got struck on the head by a golf ball. The Sporting Club was well named. You took your life in your hands on that course.

General Dawee Chulasapya, the then Deputy Prime Minister of Thailand, would often accompany us on the course. The tradition over there was that if you were a dignitary, they got you an umbrella boy. The umbrella protected the golfer from the extreme heat. I had one, too.

They were talking about building a course in Russia, in 1974, but it never got past the Kremlin. Armand Hammer, the American oilman, was involved. It was going to be designed by Robert Trent Jones, who made several trips to Russia to look over the terrain and discuss the project with Soviet leaders.

I would have loved to have played over there, but I'm not sure if they'd let me back in the country. Remember, I still owe Russia $1,200.

Speaking of Trent Jones, he and a number of leading American architects are building courses overseas. I play on them frequently. Lately I've even begun to think of myself as sort of an amateur course designer. Honestly. I could lay out a course in three hours. Build this par 3 over the water, install a trap there to catch the tee shots on the dogleg of a par 4. It's not such a big deal. Merion and Pine Valley, two of the finest courses you'll find anywhere, were both designed by amateurs who had never built another golf course. Hugh White did Merion and George Crump did Pine Valley. And what superb jobs they did.

I'm proud to say that in 1984 the Bob Hope Charity Golf Club opened in Japan. It's located about two and a half hours by car from Tokyo but the builder, a man named Zenya Hamada, has three helicopters with my likeness painted on them and it's just a twenty-minute flight from the Tokyo airport to the golf course. Maybe I'll find out what it's like to play in a kimono.

Japan is absolutely crazy about golf. They don't have enough room to build courses to accommodate all the people who want to play, so thousands of Japanese play their golf in lighted triple-deck driving ranges. I was among them on my last trip over there.

One reason golf is so popular in foreign countries is the impact made by American professionals in overseas tournaments. Ben Hogan became a legend in Scotland when he won the British Open at Carnoustie in 1953, and when Arnold Palmer started to play in the British Open every year (beginning in 1960) he was quickly followed by all the top American players.

Once the American tour ends in October the big money winners jet off to Australia, Japan and England for lucrative foreign events. In recent years the top women pros like Jan Stephenson, Nancy Lopez, JoAnne Carner, Amy Alcott and Laura Baugh have been doing the same thing. Laura is a

Arriving near the front lines in Vietnam, 1969. I've got my golf club handy, but there were no courses in Vietnam—the holes were too big.

golden goddess in Japan. She makes far more money there than she does in the United States.

The migration abroad started with the long-ago trips by my old pal Gene Sarazen, now past eighty and still playing golf nearly every day. Sarazen used to go over by boat and play exhibitions in remote places that had never seen an American golfer before. He was the pioneer in bringing American golf skills and charisma abroad.

Gene has had a wonderful career. He won the U.S. Open in 1922 when he was twenty years old. The USGA didn't know whether to give him a cup or a scooter. I don't know how much money he made in winning that Open but today it wouldn't cover the caddie fees.

But he's an unusual man, the only Italian in America who doesn't sing for a living. And when he carries a spoon, it's to take his Geritol with.

For over twenty years his great rival was Walter Hagen, the premier showman of American golf. Hagen was a marvelous player and a renowned boulevardier who loved the bright lights. One of the Haig's favorite ploys was to keep his opponent waiting on the 1st tee until he suddenly showed up in a private limo, still wearing a tuxedo.

But Sarazen got even with him at the 1932 PGA Championship in St. Paul. Hagen was late for the match, as usual, but when he finally did arrive, Sarazen wasn't there. Gene was hiding behind a concession shack and kept Hagen waiting for another ten minutes. Then he walked out and got the biggest applause of the day.

I took part in a dedication dinner one night for Gene and I still remember the windup of my speech. It went like this:

"Gene's one of a generation of professional golfers who have made a profound impact on the game internationally. It's because of the example of integrity, courtesy, good humor and true sportsmanship that they set for many years that professional golf is free of the childish, temperamental behavior that mars professional tennis. Gene and those he played with and against were just as eager to win as the pros of today but they understood that winning wasn't everything and the way you conducted yourself was just as important. Gene Sarazen is short in stature but he always walked tall."

I was thinking of Gene, and his historic rounds at St. Andrews, Carnoustie, Muirfield, Gleneagles and the other historic Scottish courses when my friend Jack Hennessy and I traveled to Scotland a few years ago for ten days of golf. We checked in at the Gleneagles Hotel and wanted to play right away. I told Jack I'd see about the luggage if he'd get us a golf cart. Jack looked at me like I'd gone daft.

"Are you kidding?" he asked. "You're from England, you should know that in Great Britain the golfers walk, not ride. Here we are in Scotland, the cradle of golf. How do you think it would look for you to be riding around like a prince?"

Jack was so persuasive that we walked, sometimes 45 holes a day. My blisters still have blisters.

The Scottish caddies are great. I get new material from them all the time. One old fellow at St. Andrews told me, "I had a golfer who was so lousy he threw his clubs into the water. Then he dived in himself. I thought he was going to drown, but I remembered he couldn't keep his head down long enough."

The weather over there is always, of course, capricious at best. Wind, rain and bone-chilling sleet. And fog. One day at St. Andrews my caddie lost three balls—on the 1st tee.

Another caddie was working for a golfer whose ball had stopped near the edge of a lake. The golfer hit the shot and when he followed through too far, he tumbled into the water. As the golfer was going down for the third time he had one hand sticking out of the water. The caddie nudged the other caddie in the group and said, "I think he wants a 5-iron."

Thirteen

The Skins Game: Baring Golf's Future

Looking down the road, I can see only good things for golf. It's growing all the time. New tournaments and new players, mixing in with the established events and the older stars. Golf is very fortunate in that it has been able to maintain its historic traditions while taking on innovations that create more interest and additional excitement.

An example would be the Skins Game, a $360,000 shoot-out held for the first time on Thanksgiving weekend in 1983 and again in 1984 at the Desert Highlands course that Jack Nicklaus designed in Scottsdale, Arizona. It had only four participants—Nicklaus, Arnold Palmer, Gary Player and Tom Watson.

Each hole was played as a separate contest for a certain amount of money, starting with $10,000 on the 1st hole and escalating to $30,000 for each of the last 6. If a hole were tied by any two or more players, the pot would carry over into the next hole. Pretty soon it's palm-sweating time.

I watched both the Skins Game on television and I think it's great for golf. Something fresh, with lots of immediate drama. In a regular tour event you watch it over four rounds, waiting for the winner to be determined late Sunday afternoon. But in the Skins, from the moment they start, someone wins $10,000, and the excitement blasts right off, and the next thing you know they're teeing it up for $30,000.

When I first heard about the Skins Game I expected to see a match between Telly Savalas, Don Rickles and Alan Cranston. The Skins Game . . . it sound like golf at a nudist camp. But it's a dream game for the pros. Gambling without using your own money. The four who played were all joking, laughing and having fun. When I'm playing for a $2.00 nassau I look like I'm in the middle of open heart surgery. My knees shake so much I feel like I'm auditioning for *Flashdance*.

Actually it's a game that every golfer can relate to, because we've all played a lower-keyed variation of it, usually for $1.00 a hole with carryovers. We can understand and appreciate the pressure those four pros were competing in.

I'll never forget the look on Palmer's face in 1983 when he knocked in that putt for $100,000. He jumped around and clapped and cheered. He was ecstatic. After all the great golf he has played, here was a fresh note in his career and he made more money with that putt than he had ever made in a single tournament.

Arnold didn't play all that well in the two days of competition—he was in the cactus and the rocks half the time, it seemed, but he made the crucial thirty-five-foot putt on a carryover hole. I told him later that he made $140,000 for two days of golf and was never in the fairway.

You remember what happened toward the end of the match. Watson thought he saw Player extract a piece of crabgrass as he was positioning his ball for a chip shot. Tom didn't say anything about it at the time, but after it was over he accosted Player in the parking lot at Desert Highlands and accused him of violating a rule. Playing for that kind of money got to all the golfers. Player didn't mean to move the sprig of grass. Anything that was green they try to put in their pocket.

Player made $150,000 on one hole. I get goose bumps when I find a dime that someone's left in a pay phone. And he made $170,000 in the tournament. That's not bad for a day of gardening. For that kind of money I'd chew trees down with my teeth.

That was some battle they had in 1984, too. Tom Watson won everything the first day and pocketed $120,000. On the second day, with higher stakes, it all boiled down to the last hole. Nicklaus sank an 8-foot putt for the only birdie on the hole and collected $240,000. Of course, remember that he had to pay his green fees out of that. But $240,000! That's enough money to take your whole family to a Michael Jackson concert. That's too much money. I get mad when I lose the dime I use as a ball marker.

Can you imagine getting $240,000 for one day's work? Who does Nicklaus think he is—a basketball player? He's the first one to take that much money out of a hole in the ground . . . who isn't an Arab.

Watching it on TV, I tried to put myself in the situation of the four players. If I had an 8-foot putt for $240,000, I'd probably miss it. I'd probably even miss the 16-footer coming back. But those fellows are accustomed to that kind of pressure. They put on a great show, and the second time around they didn't have any grass problems.

But at least golfers just move plants. Other athletes are smoking them. Golfers don't take drugs. It would be too obvious. The alligator on their shirts would roll over on its back. You just can't take drugs and play golf at the same time. It's hard enough to hit that ball when it's standing still. Can you imagine if there was as much drug use in golf as there is in other sports? PGA would stand for Pot Growers of America. The tour has a simple test to see if a player is on drugs—if Isao Aoki speaks and the player understands him, he's on something. Consider the consequences if the heavy hitters on tour took steroids. It would be the first time golf balls were ever tracked by NASA.

No, the tour doesn't have to worry about that. I asked the commissioner, Deane Beman, what the chances were of the tour developing a drug problem. He said, "About the same as the chances of Gary Player and Tom Watson sharing a cabin on 'Love Boat.' "

But I can't wait until they set up a Skins Game for comedians. I might have a chance with Uncle Miltie using the ladies' tee and Don Rickles trying to hit a hockey puck.

Another area where golf has been very fortunate has been in the makeup of its leading players. Golf's great stars have all been ideal role models for the young people of America to look up to. This is very important. These stars have served as wonderful examples for others to emulate, not only in

Arnie misses a crucial birdie putt in the Skins Game. Either that or his tractor wouldn't start.

Gary Player sinks it for $150,000 on the seventeenth hole of the Skins Game. Americans have always been generous in the area of foreign aid.

their performance and sportsmanship on the course but in the way they have conducted their lives.

Nicklaus is the epitome of the awesomely talented gentleman golfer, with a head on his shoulders and both feet on the ground. He has transformed himself from a tiger into a pussycat. (It's amazing what $200,000 here and there can do.) Now when Jack talks, E. F. Hutton listens.

Johnny Miller is the quintessential family man, very much at home on his farm in Utah. When he was 49 strokes under par in those successive tournaments at Phoenix and Tucson in 1975, I thought he would tear the tour apart. John has done very well, but he has always placed family before golf and has never displayed that fierce hunger to stay out and grind away on the tournament scene week after week.

Miller did go over to South Africa a few years ago, however, and won a nifty $500,000 in a challenge match after a 9-hole sudden-death play-off with Seve Ballesteros. Miller, Nicklaus and Trevino won a total of $740,000 in that tournament. It's about time Americans got some foreign aid for a change. Johnny stayed over an extra day, negotiating to buy Africa.

Following that tournament here at home, I was really intrigued by it. They were playing for all that money in the middle of the bush country. It was an interesting course they played. The head pro was Tarzan. They had some dangerous hazards, too. On the par-3 holes, you had to hit over a tribe of pygmies with blowguns. If you're over the green, you're OK. But if you're short, your hat size shrinks down to a one and five-eighths.

At the same time they were showing the world how to play championship golf with a smile, those star players were becoming corporate tycoons. They all have their own companies with managers, agents, tax consultants and TV advisers. They're making so much money their golf bags have special compartments just to hold all the cash.

Palmer used to be a professional golfer, but now he's a conglomerate. He has so many irons in the fire he has to play the tour with his woods. Can you believe all the TV commercials Arnie does? He has the same slogan as Mr. Whipple, only his is "Please don't squeeze the money." Arnie also promotes a dictating machine. I bought one and it's really something. You record your voice and he talks back to you.

There's one commercial that shows Arnie running on the golf course in a jogging suit. I don't know whether he's exercising or looking for his ball.

When I received the Old Tom Morris Award a couple of years ago from the Golf Course Superintendents Association of America, Arnie, who had been the recipient the year previously, was the presenter. I got to the hotel in Las Vegas for the ceremony and I knew Arnie was already there, because I saw his tractor in the parking lot. Palmer was not in a real good mood that day. He had seen a commercial on TV that he wasn't in.

But seriously, I think it's great that our star golfers are involved in so many commercial enterprises, including TV commercials. It's good for

You think the big boys don't feel the pressure in a competition like the Skins Game? here's Nicklaus after a rimmed putt, reacting as though his American Express contract had been cancelled.

Here's Arnie swinging away in the Skins Game, watched closely by Rules Chairman Joe Dey, Nicklaus, Player, and Watson. They invited me to make it a fivesome, but Arnie wanted too many strokes.

them and good for golf. They've certainly earned it. But I sometimes wonder if Palmer isn't getting too involved with TV commercials. When he missed a putt the other day, he put the ball back and said, "Take two."

The earlier legends of golf didn't have this opportunity. Byron Nelson, for example, was a great champion who was born forty years too early. I was sitting with him at dinner in Jim Chambers' home in Dallas recently when he mentioned that in 1945, when he won nineteen tournaments and *eleven in a row*, he didn't make as much money that entire year as first place pays in a tournament today.

That's because when Byron was winning all those events, there was no television. TV is a powerful force in golf today. The rights money it pays enables sponsors to keep raising their purses, to $400,000 and $500,000 and $600,000, and still donate handsome sums to charities. Each tournament gets certain proceeds from television, 43 percent of its purse if it is on network TV and 37 percent of the purse if it is not.

This can occasionally create problems. In the Nabisco Dinah Shore tournament in 1984 the women were playing so fast that they were asked to wait six minutes on the tee at a point late in the telecast. Pat Bradley was on the 17th tee in the final round, leading by a shot. After the wait she began spraying her shots all over the course, ultimately losing to Juli Inkster in a play-off.

Working closely with the NBC people who televise my tournament in Palm Springs, I can see that they do an excellent job. Don Ohlmeyer, who ran NBC sports for several years and now has his own highly successful communications company, created some great filmed features. Larry Cirillo, NBC's coordinating producer, is a thorough professional in every aspect of his work. It isn't easy. Golf is the hardest of all the sports to televise, but it's improving every year and the growing ratings reflect the widespread interest in golf.

Sometimes the networks have tried wiring the players—placing a little mike on them—and this hasn't always proved successful. It's live, remember, and there's no way to delete a bleep when a player hits a bad shot. Golfers do have their own language.

Stadium Golf, conceived by Deane Beman and the PGA Tour, is a great innovation. The new courses on which the tour events are being played are built for spectators, with hilly vantage points and bleachers behind the greens. They can accommodate a far larger gallery that way. In five years I look for golf galleries on the tour to double in size.

More people are not only watching golf, they're playing the game. The most recent figures say that the sale of golf equipment in the United States in one year is $270 million.

Byron Nelson Classic, Dallas, 1973. I always like to drive my own golf cart in the pro-ams. That way I can set my own pace for signing autographs, and when my golf game goes lousy I can get out of town in a hurry.

216

When a golfer can win $144,000 in a tournament, as Fred Couples did in the Tournament Players Championship in 1984, you know the game has become big business. So big that there is not much levity out there now. Instead of partying at night the players are practicing putting on their hotel room carpets.

But they do get out together once in a while. Dolores and I invite all the players, along with about two hundred other guests, to a party at our home in Palm Springs during the Desert Classic. The veranda has an open roof, and one night it started to rain. J. C. Snead looked around and declared, "This place reminds me of my ranch down in Texas except that the roof don't leak."

Billy Casper is known to some as a rather phlegmatic person, but in 1982 at San Diego he told me the story about a golfer who was playing in the rain. The water was up to his knees and along came a rowboat and a voice asked, "Can I help you?"

The golfer replied, "No, I made a deal with God."

The rains were soon up to the golfer's chest and along came a helicopter and a voice said, "Can I help you?"

"No, I made a deal with God."

The water was soon over the golfer's head, and he drowned. When he got to heaven, the golfer ran into God and asked, "What happened to our deal."

God said, "I don't know—I sent a rowboat and a helicopter for you."

The senior tour is another example of golf's mushrooming expansion and Billy Casper, approaching fifty a few years ago, realized that here could be a lucrative extension of his career. Except at that point he didn't have much of a career. His game had turned sour. He was hitting the ball so wildly he couldn't make a cut, so he decided to do something about it.

First he saw a hypnotist who stressed the value of positive thinking, of concentrating upon visualizing the proper shot instead of worrying about the improper one, and then he rebuilt his swing. From a lifelong "fader," hitting the ball slightly left to right, he developed an effective right-to-left ball flight. Billy became a champion again, and in 1983 he won the U.S. Senior Open.

You can't discuss the tremendous growth of golf without including the women pros. Behind the aggressive leadership first of Commissioner Ray Volpe and then Volpe's successor, John Laupheimer, the gals have gone from playing for lunch money to $9 million annually. That's terrific, because I can easily remember the day when the women's purse was a purse.

Yes, the gals have really come a long way, and they're looking great, too. Not too long ago the ball was the only object on the course with dimples. I really enjoy playing with them, but how can I keep my head down when there's so much to look at?

No matter how you look at it, the game of golf has never been in better shape.

Epilogue

So much has happened in golf since the hardcover version of this book came out in the spring of 1985 that the editors of Doubleday suggested an additional chapter, an epilogue if you will, for the paperback. I thought it was a good idea, too. I was pleased with the reception the book received. Even the critics liked it, which proved they weren't carrying over any grudges from my last picture.

We'll all look back on 1986 as a momentous year in golf. It was a year in which the old-timers really had their inning. Jack Nicklaus wins the Masters and Raymond Floyd wins the U.S. Open, the oldest champions ever in those tournaments. And there were other stars too! Greg Norman wins the British Open and leads all four of the major championships going into the final round. Bob Tway explodes out of the sand on the 72d hole into the cup for a birdie to win the PGA Championship, the most incredible thing I've ever seen in golf. When he saw the ball roll in, Tway jumped up and down as though he had just signed for a Toyota commercial. What a shot! But Tway goes into those traps with such confidence. When I go in, I bring along two days of provisions and a change of linen.

It was great to see the older guys doing so well. Soon you'll see players using their reading glasses to putt. Actually, golf is like sex—you can go on forever, providing they let you ride a cart.

I watched the Masters on television and I just couldn't believe the way Nicklaus putted over those last 10 holes. He made everything with that new oversized putter that his company, MacGregor, had manufactured for him. As I sat there I thought, "Where can I get a putter like that?" I was only one of fifty thousand who went out and bought one.

A couple of days later I called Jack to congratulate him. I told him that some of the younger players were upset—not only was Jack shooting his age, he was shooting theirs, too. Nicklaus has offered me a lot of golf tips over the years, so I asked him what I'd need to hit a 250-yard drive and he said a 100-yard roll. Jack's doing very well financially, too. He stopped counting his money about the same time I stopped counting my strokes. The truth is that Nicklaus has been winning big since he found out what social security pays.

What was really exciting about the Masters was that Jack, at forty-six, broke one of golf's oldest traditions: the first thing a veteran player loses is his putting. Ben Hogan would still be great today if he could putt. But Jack proved he hadn't lost his touch. I hadn't seen him putt like that since he beat Lee Elder in that marathon play-off for the American Golf Classic championship at Firestone in 1968. This was Jack's sixth Masters title, and he had the world pulling for him.

This one is a real collector's item from the 1986 golf season. You seldom see the four major championship winners of the year together. I offered them a little advice on swing technique and there they are: Jack Nicklaus (Masters), Bob Tway (PGA), Raymond Floyd (U.S. Open) and Greg Norman (British Open).

Considering all the times in recent years when he was in position to win but couldn't quite pull it off, Jack had this one coming to him. It's like the Academy Awards. If an actor gives a great performance and doesn't win, and then gets nominated again the following year, he's got a lot of people rooting for him.

When a forty-six-year-old guy wins the Masters, they should call it the Prune Juice Open. There's no question that older people prefer golf over tennis. In tennis, there's no love after forty.

Floyd's victory in the Open at Shinnecock Hills was just about as dramatic. I'd played Shinnecock once, several years ago, and the rough did me in. When you hit a ball into that stuff, you need a tetanus shot. Nicklaus discovered that on the 10th hole of the opening round, when he lost his ball and three hundred people couldn't find it. Of course, conditions that day were impossible. Cold, wind and heavy rain. I was surprised a man of Floyd's age would even venture out in it on a day like that.

But those hardy old-timers don't worry about getting off the tee. The big problem is getting the tee in the ground. Just the other day I cut my ball and my caddie repaired it with Polygrip. Golf knows no age, but you know you're getting on when your score begins to look like your social security number.

Lee Trevino played marvelously in the U.S. Open. The weather in the first round must have reminded him of the day he got struck by lightning at the 1975 Western Open in Chicago. They say lightning never strikes the same place twice, but Lee took no chances at Shinnecock. He was wearing asbestos shorts. You have to remember that when lightning hits Mexican food, something has to give.

Trevino was cleaning the windows of his home in Dallas one day when a woman stopped by and asked him, "Could you possibly clean the windows of my house? I'll pay you more than that woman does." Lee thought about that for a moment and then replied, "That might be difficult because I sleep with the lady in this house."

The old boys had their year, that's true, but there is some fabulous younger talent in golf these days, too. Greg Norman, Steve Ballesteros, Bernhard Langer and Bob Tway come to mind. The way that Tway won the PGA out of the bunker was, as Nicklaus said, just unbelievable. Afterward, on television, Tway had tears in his eyes. That's the way I am after I wake up and discover it was all a fantasy. You had to feel sorry for Norman, who had led all the way. I know how he felt. I had the same feeling many times at the Academy Awards ceremony. But Norman proved what a class act is by walking over immediately and shaking Tway's hand. When Greg goes home for a visit to Australia they'll probably knight him, because they are really crazy about golf and he's a wonderful ambassador for the game.

Two old friends recounting a lot of good times together. Is this what they call the interlocking grip?

Incidentally, have you noticed how the foreign players are coming on strong in American golf? Norman, Ballesteros, Langer, Ian Woosnam of Wales, Sandy Lyle of Scotland, Tommy Nakajima from Japan. The British team beat the Americans in the 1985 Ryder Cup, and the next year the British women amateurs whipped the Americans in the Curtis Cup. What are the British putting in their tea these days?

Of course, it helps that the British can now select their Ryder Cup teams from throughout the continent of Europe. That gave them Ballesteros and Langer. There's a guy from Sweden named Ove Sellberg who will soon join them. Sellberg won the Epson Grand Prix of Europe in 1986 and became the first Swedish player to receive an invitation for the World Series of Golf. One day you might even see a Russian on that team.

I'm looking forward to the Ryder Cup in 1987, at Nicklaus's course, Muirfield Village in Dublin, Ohio. For the first time in thirty years the Americans may be the underdogs. I'll be there, and I'll feel right at home. After all, I'm an international player. I can say "shank" in twenty-seven languages.

But I was sorry to read about the prolonged sparring match between Commissioner Deane Beman and Ballesteros and Mac O'Grady. I can't say who's right and who's wrong; it's just unfortunate when talent like that encounters problems. I remember both Ballesteros and O'Grady from playing at Lakeside in North Hollywood, my home course. In 1980, after Ballesteros won the Masters, his manager at that time, Ed Barner of Los Angeles, brought Steve out to Lakeside. He played three or four holes with various groups of members, and was very pleasant.

Tournament golf is a great game, but the pressures are becoming so great they can turn the players old in a hurry. I remember when kids used to drive by a golf course and yell "Sissy!" at the players. Now they realize, after watching on television, the terror of a four-foot downhill putt for $50,000. The money, though, can soothe those frazzled nerves. It's like show business—you've got to learn to absorb the highs and the lows without cracking. My psychiatrist can explain all that.

I doubt if he could explain this nutty fascination I have with golf. After all these years, I'm still hopelessly hooked on the game. I play or practice nearly every day. My Lakeside handicap has remained at 20 although, like most golfers, I think I could reduce that by at least a couple of strokes if I could get a few putts to drop.

Over the past few years I've lost a little distance on my long game, which probably isn't surprising for a guy of eighty-three. Tom Watson once told me, "If you had a short game, you could score." Well, I've got a pretty good short game now, but my long game has deteriorated.

Since all the disclosures and controversy about athletes on drugs, I've detected some telltale signs in several caddies I've had. The other day one of them kept my score on Zig Zag paper. I asked him, "Where is the pin?" He said, "I don't know, I'll check it when it comes around again."

That was too much. I said, "Don't you know that stuff will ruin your nostrils?" He just laughed and replied, "Who cares, man, I've got three of them."

Personally I don't take anything on the golf course, although some of my opponents would like to inject me with truth serum.

Golf has a way of enslaving us. Jim Chambers, a friend of mine in Dallas, loves the game. His wife once told him he had hoof and mouth disease. "You walk all day," she said, "and you talk about it all night."

It's funny what a guy will do to get in a round of golf. A couple of years ago I was doing a show in Merryville, Indiana. The sponsors of the Vince Lombardi Memorial tournament in Milwaukee asked me to participate, so they sent a plane to Merryville and picked me up. I played 18 holes, got up on a podium to exchange a few jokes with Bart Starr, then flew back to Merryville in time to have a quick dinner and go on stage that night.

But maybe the years are catching up with me. In the summer of 1986 I was appearing for a week at the Fox Theater in Atlanta. I had wanted to play on a Monday morning at Capital City, a great old course in Atlanta where Bing Crosby, Ed Dudley, Bobby Dodd and I had some lively games thirty years ago. The course is normally closed on Mondays, but they said they'd have a cart waiting and an assistant pro to play with me.

Well, for some reason, I told my limousine driver that morning to take me to Peachtree, another fine Atlanta course that Robert Trent Jones had built, with Bobby Jones, in 1948. When I arrived at Peachtree, the pro shop was locked up. A woman came out of the office to see what I wanted. I said, "Where's the golf cart and the assistant pro?" The woman had no idea what I was talking about, but she called Dick Murphy, the head pro, at his home. Dick hurried out, and while we were waiting, I told my wife, Dolores, "You know, I think we're at the wrong place." When Dick arrived, I explained the situation. We stayed and played 9 holes, and later I called Capital City to apologize for the mix-up.

That was the week I also forgot to introduce the governor of Georgia, Joe Frank Harris, who was in the audience with his wife one night. I called him the next day and he said, "Don't give it a thought, Bob; we really enjoyed the show." He's a classy guy. Later I received a dozen golf balls from him in the mail.

Appearing in Atlanta reminded me of the time several years ago when I played in the pro-am of the Atlanta Classic. On the practice tee that day I was having trouble hitting the ball. Gardner Dickinson, a fine golf teacher and an excellent player although he couldn't have weighed much over 130 pounds, walked over to have a look. I said, "How are you doing, 1-iron?" Gardner ignored the crack and advised me to get my legs into the shot. On

I always like to warm up, just like the pros, before teeing off. Sometimes you can even learn something from your neighbor on the tee. It's good to know that even Jack Nicklaus needs to work out the kinks.

the front nine, with Nicklaus as my pro, I shot 38. Coming in, it looked like we had a chance to win. On the 18th hole, a par 5, Nicklaus went for the green with his second shot and knocked it into the water. I hit my third shot on the green and made a thirty-foot downhill putt for a natural birdie and net eagle that won the pro-am for our team.

I still think I'm playing as well now as I did before. The only difference is I need two or three guys to replace my divots.

One of my favorite golf resorts in the world is Gleneagles, in Scotland, with its beautiful Kings and Queens courses. Ian Marchbank, the club pro, watched me take a practice swing and gently said, "I think you belong on the Queens course."

Ian should have been with me that day last year when I had six pars on 10 holes at Lakeside. If I could maintain that pace over 18 I'd achieve my lifetime goal and shoot my age.

In 1985 I flew over to Miyasaki, on the southern tip of Japan, for the Dunlop Phoenix tournament, which attracts most of the leading American pros. Miyasaki was like Palm Springs, sunny and warm. The tournament had named the pro-am for me. Now they're building courses in China. That's all we need: take-out golf.

Golf continues to expand in England. Some of those London golf clubs are very exclusive. One won't even accept actors—and they keep asking me to join.

It's always a pleasure, and an honor, to play Walter Annenberg's course in Palm Springs. That course, which gets action only when Walter feels like playing, is so well maintained it has a maid. The first time I played there it was with Walter, Ike and Freeman Gosden. I took a huge divot and started to replace it. Walter came over to me and said, "Don't worry about it." He had a man standing on a high ridge who came down whenever a player took a divot and sewed them back in.

I don't know about you, but I'm investing my money in miniature golf. I think it's coming back. I ought to know—I've been playing it the last few years.

But I'm always working on my game. While on a fund-raising tour recently for the Penn State football program we did shows in Hershey, Pittsburgh and Philadelphia. I played the East Course at Merion, which has held so many national championships. Bill Papa, the starter on the West Course, was watching me. "Stay down on the ball just a fraction longer," Papa told me, and it worked. I started hitting the ball well again. Bill might have told the same thing to Greg Norman before Greg pushed his 4-iron shot to the green on the final hole of the 1986 Masters, when a par would have tied Nicklaus.

One of the reporters on that Penn State tour asked me what I shot. "I shoot anything," I told him. "Anything. I'm like Jerry Ford. I shoot anything that gets in the way."

I had an opportunity on the tour to spend some time with Joe Paterno, Penn State's head football coach. Paterno is one of the outstanding coaches of all time. Coaching a major college football team is a tough job. Joe didn't know whether he had enjoyed his honeymoon until he saw the films.

The only reason I don't play more golf is because I'm working nearly all the time. I average about a hundred stage shows a year, plus the NBC television shows, commercials, the TV productions my company does and various other projects.

In the summer of 1986 I was one of twelve immigrants given the Medal of Liberty at the Statue of Liberty celebration on Governors Island. The first time I saw the Statue of Liberty was when I was four years old. She was six. This time I noticed some changes in the old girl. She was looking to the shore from the New York side, but she was mooning New Jersey. On the night of the televised ceremony, I was scheduled to do a show later, at 11:30, on the boat *Princess New York* in the harbor. The Navy had made all the arrangements. They barraged me with communiques and confirmations of communiques. The orders were very explicit: Leave the stage at Governors Island at 10:15 P.M. and a launch would be waiting to take me out to the boat at 10:25. I hurried off the stage at the prescribed time, got to the launch and asked, "Are we ready?" There was a moment or two of silence and then a Navy man said, "There's only one problem. The motor won't work."

Our Navy? Can you believe that? I knew they were waiting for me on the ship. Luckily, another launch, which had brought Dolores and Walter Annenberg to the program, was available, and I got there on time.

Earlier that summer I was flying in my own plane from Burbank Airport down to the Miramar Naval Air Station in San Diego to do a televised tribute for the ninetieth birthday of General James Doolittle, who led an American bombing mission over Tokyo during the early days of World War II in 1942. It was to be a short flight, only about twenty-five minutes. I was reading a script and not paying much attention to the route when the pilot came on and announced we were heading back to Burbank. I didn't know what was going on. After we landed, the pilot came back and said, "We're having some trouble with the motor." I got off the plane and the television cameras were rolling. The pilot had called the tower to tell them about the motor, and we had to make a forced landing. As soon as the pilot had notified the tower, they sent out the fire department, which was a good thing because the motor was smoking. Within a few minutes the news had gone around the world.

It was a busy summer. Later in the year I flew commercially to Cleveland to visit a relative and was driven down to Columbus for the national convention of the Fraternal Order of the Eagles. The Eagles and I have had a close relationship for fifteen years. They are the most charitable organization in existence. They contribute money to the Eisenhower Medical Center and also help support a high school for crippled children in Port Arthur, Texas. So whenever they have their annual convention, I join them and do some shows.

I went to the Montana State Fair in Billings and then played in Jerry Ford's golf tournament with the tour pros in Vail, Colorado, before going on to Akron, Ohio, to receive the Ambassador of Golf award from the World Series of Golf. Then it was up to Alaska for a week of fishing and a few rounds of golf at the Eagleglen course on the Elmendorf Air Force base in Anchorage.

President Ford joined me for the pro-am in Akron and it was a fun week. I always enjoy getting together with him. When Ford played football at Michigan, some people say he never wore a helmet. Now he plays golf and his entire gallery wears helmets. He was a center who was never too accurate with his snaps. He made runners out of his punters.

During the pro-am in Akron, Ford asked me if I had seen much lately of President Ronald Reagan. I reminded him that Reagan doesn't play much golf, just once a year with Walter Annenberg. Reagan is widely remembered for his role of George Gipp, the great halfback, in the movie *Knute Rockne— All American*. In the action scenes he was so shifty there was never any doubt that he would go into politics.

In the Rockne movie the action was rough and tough, with plenty of hard hitting. Reagan came out of it all right, but his stand-in suffered three concussions.

I still spend part of each winter in Palm Springs. The place amazes me the way it's grown since I first started going there. Golf courses are springing up everywhere. One of the major reasons for this is the aggressive management of the Landmark Land Company, run by a couple of ex-golfers named Ernie Vossler and Joe Walser. Landmark started at the LaQuinta Golf and Tennis Resort, spilled over to Mission Hills and now has a gigantic complex mushrooming at PGA West in LaQuinta that will eventually wind up with seven golf courses.

Pete Dye designed the Stadium Course at PGA West for tournament golf, and it's no secret that our Bob Hope Chrysler Classic (we just added the corporate name) may add that site to its tournament rotation. I rode around the course recently with Deane Beman, the tour commissioner. Frankly, it looked a bit difficult for the average amateur player. There are some holes where you could lose a ball, caddie and foursome.

One day I was making plans over the phone to play a benefit round for the USO in Palm Springs. I asked where the outing would be and they said

Sharing a laugh with President Ford over the pink golf ball he gave me at the World Series of Golf pro-am. I told him I'd use it on the gay tee.

at the Desert Princess. I said, "Where the hell is that?" Well, I found it, not far off Highway 111, and it was incredible. They have a beautiful golf course, a 300-room hotel and 345 acres of property. It all looks as if it had just sprung out of the sand.

Indian Wells is building two first-class municipal courses, with a pair of major hotels, on land I had once bought for my kids. They had it for twenty years, sold it and now it's going to become golf property. I owe it to myself to play there.

One of the hazards of living in California is the periodic threat of earthquakes. California has a lot of them. Where else can you see whitecaps in your martini? Palm Springs has acquired a new name—Shake and Bake. I never dreamed that my homes in Palm Springs and North Hollywood would wind up across the street from each other. One night my zip code changed three times while I was still in bed.

Between earthquakes I enjoyed watching the televised wedding ceremony of Prince Andrew and Sarah Ferguson. You've never seen such luxury. The settings made "Lifestyles of the Rich and Famous" look like the Beverly Hillbillies. But somehow the name "Fergie" doesn't sound like a princess. It sounds more like a relief pitcher for the Dodgers.

It was the most romantic wedding since Boy George married himself. The closest that Americans would get to royalty like that would be if Burger King merged with Dairy Queen. Prince Andrew and I have something in common. Whenever Dolores's relatives stay overnight, I'm also fourth in line for the throne.

But I digress. It's time to head over to Lakeside for another round of golf. I know I'll shoot a good score because now I'm using an orthopedic putter. I'm shooting my age consistently these days, but nobody believes I'm 108.